Ghana National Health Insurance Scheme

A WORLD BANK STUDY

Ghana National Health Insurance Scheme

Improving Financial Sustainability Based on Expenditure Review

Huihui Wang, Nathaniel Otoo, and Lydia Dsane-Selby

WORLD BANK GROUP

ISBN (paper): 978-1-4648-1117-3
ISBN (electronic): 978-1-4648-1118-0
DOI: 10.1596/978-1-4648-1117-3

Cover design: Debra Naylor, Naylor Design, Inc.

Library of Congress Cataloging-in-Publication Data

Contents

Boxes

Figures

Tables

Acknowledgments

Huihui Wang (Senior Economist, World Bank) led the preparation of this report from the World Bank. The team greatly appreciates the collaboration of the Ghana National Health Insurance Authority led by Nathaniel Otoo (Chief Executive). The team gratefully acknowledges the valuable guidance and support provided by Henry Kerali (Country Director), Kathleen Beegle (Program Leader) and Trina Haque (Practice Manager). The report benefited from the insightful comments offered by its peer reviewers, including Laurence Lannes (Senior Economist), Moulay Driss (Senior Economist), Christoph Kurowski (Lead Health Specialist), and Francisca Akala (Senior Health Specialist). This team is grateful for the administrative assistance provided by Stephen Tettevie and Sariette Jippe.

About the Authors

Huihui Wang is a senior economist in the Health, Nutrition, and Population Global Practice at the World Bank. She has almost 20 years of experiences working in low-, middle-, and high-income countries, with a focus on supporting them to achieve universal health coverage. She leads the World Bank's technical support in health system reforms of various countries, including public financing, health insurance, service delivery, and quality of care. She was appointed by the president of Ghana as a member of the Technical Review Committee for the reform of the Ghana National Health Insurance Scheme. Her responsibilities in the World Bank also include preparing, supervising, and evaluating lending operations at the country level. Before joining the World Bank, she was a researcher on health sector reform initiatives in China and the United States. Huihui has a multidisciplinary background that makes her a competent player in global health field: a medical degree from Beijing Medical University, an MA in economics, and a PhD in health services and policy analysis from the University of California, Berkeley. She has extensive teaching experience to executives, mid-career professionals, graduate students, and undergraduates through lectures at Peking University; the University of California, Berkeley; and the World Bank.

Nathaniel Otoo worked for over 10 years with Ghana's National Health Insurance Authority. In 2015, he became Chief Executive of the Authority, a position he held until February 2017. His previous work experience spanned the social security, manufacturing, and trade promotion sectors. He holds a bachelor's degree in law from the University of Ghana, a professional law qualification, and master's degree in international relations from the International University of Japan. Nathaniel is a founding member of the Joint Learning Network for Universal Health Coverage. In 2013, he became the network's first convener, a position he held for 2 years. Nathaniel has contributed to and participated in numerous universal health coverage activities and events around the world. He is currently an independent consultant.

Lydia Dsane-Selby is Deputy Chief Executive of Operations of the Ghana National Health Insurance Authority. She was Director of Claims since May 2013. Previously she was Director of Clinical Audit for 4 years. She has 10 years of experience with the organization, including as Medical Advisor in the

Research and Development Directorate. She has played an integral part in several key innovations: the development of the diagnosis-related group payment mechanism, the development of the accreditation tools and process, the introduction of clinical audits with the development of tools and a manual, and the introduction of e-claims with business rules for cost containment. Before joining the Ghana National Health Insurance Authority, she was Medical Officer at Korle-Bu Teaching Hospital, Achimota Hospital, and in the United Kingdom. She was a speaker at several international conferences on health insurance fraud and abuse and strategic purchasing.

Abbreviations

CHAG   Christian Health Association of Ghana
DHS   Demography and Health Survey
DRG   diagnosis-related group
FFS   fee-for-service
GDGR   Ghana diagnosis-related group
GH¢   Ghanaian cedi
MMR   maternal mortality rate
NHIA   National Health Insurance Authority
NHIS   National Health Insurance Scheme
SSA   Sub-Saharan Africa
SSNIT   Social Security and National Insurance Trust
TFR   total fertility rate
U5M   under-five mortality
VAT   value-added tax

CHAPTER 1

Introduction

Background

Since the establishment of Ghana National Health Insurance Scheme (NHIS) in 2003, the Government of Ghana has made substantial progress toward its goal of universal health care. As of 2014, the NHIS covered 10.5 million people, or 40 percent of Ghana's population. The total number of inpatient and outpatient visits to health facilities rose from just under 0.5 per capita in 2005 to almost 3 per capita in 2014.

The Ghana National Health Insurance Authority (NHIA) has strengthened its technical capacities over time, developing highly competent professional teams in the fields of actuarial sciences, financial management, insurance mechanisms, and health financing. Building robust actuarial-analysis capacity is crucial to safeguarding the NHIA's financial sustainability. In addition, a clinical audit division was created in 2009 to review the authenticity of claims and reduce fraud. The government established four claims processing centers to centralize the claims processing, and with support from the Ghana Health Insurance Project (2007–14) the Accra center now also allows for claims to be submitted and processed electronically. A revised NHIS medicine list was introduced to promote rational prescribing practices. The authorities shifted provider payments for inpatient services from a fee-for-service model to Ghana Diagnosis-related-groups (GDRG). A system of capitation[1] payment for primary outpatient care was launched in the Ashanti region in 2012 and is currently being rolled out in other regions.

Despite the government's efforts, ensuring the NHIS's financial sustainability continues to pose a serious challenge and remains authorities' priority. Total claims payments rose from just GH¢7.6 million in 2005 to over GH¢1.07 billion in 2014. Meanwhile, the NHIS's annual deficit reached GH¢300 million. In September 2015, the Minister of Health commissioned a seven-member technical committee to review the NHIS. This was the first of such efforts since the establishment of NHIS. The review assessed the state of the NHIS and proposed measures to sustain the scheme.

Objective

This study's goal is to inform policy makers on improving financial sustainability of the NHIS based on quantitative evidence of claim expenditure patterns. The study generates quantitative evidence on patterns of claims expenditures. It also offers insights into how to strengthen country systems for making evidence-based policies in health sector in general and NHIS in particular.

Focusing on expenditure side will be crucial to NHIS's financial sustainability over both the short and long term. In the short term, the difficulty of raising additional revenue in the current macro-fiscal context[2] underscores the importance of efficient spending to control the deficit. In the long term, a persistent focus on efficient spending will enable the authorities to address evolving challenges in health financing. The international experience shows that even high-income countries have difficulty accommodating the rising health care expenditure. Appropriate policies for more efficient spending are crucial to the efficiency, equity and sustainability of health insurance schemes of countries at all income levels.

Designing policies that reflect Ghana's unique circumstances requires precise and detailed evidence. To maximize their effectiveness, the NHIS reform efforts must target key policy areas, and limited data on the efficiency and equity of NHIS service provision represents a serious obstacle to effective policymaking. The country's capacity to generate reliable, up-to-date evidence will be crucial to ensure continued financial stability of NHIS as the dynamics between NHIS, service providers and members inevitably change over time.

Methodology and Data

This study's methodological approach combines elements of a quantitative analysis and a desk review. The study examines the NHIS's basic features and its role in health financing. A statistical analysis at the service-provider and member levels reveals patterns in claims expenditure, highlighting key factors affecting the level and efficiency of NHIS claims expenditures.

The study draws on national health-sector data and NHIS data, as well as data specific to the Volta region. National-level data include the fiscal accounts from the Ministry of Finance, the consolidated accounts from the Ghana Revenue Authority, annual reports from the NHIS and Ghana Health Services, summary statistics from NHIS financial statements, NHIS membership reports, and the Ghana Demography and Health Surveys (DHSs) for 2008 and 2014. Volta-specific data include claims summaries,[3] NHIS membership data, a list of credential facilities, and the diagnosis-related-groups (DRG) tariff list, all from 2014 (table 1.1).

The Volta region was selected for an in-depth expenditure analysis. Due to data constraints, an analysis for each region was not possible. These constraints are less binding in the Volta region, as it is one of two regions in which all claims

Table 1.1 Data Sources

Data source	Period	Key information
National-level data		
The fiscal accounts from the Ministry of Finance	2010–14	Total government spending from the statutory fund, the National Health Fund, and ministries, departments and agencies
The consolidated accounts of the Ghana Revenue Authority	2011–14	Spending by the Ministry of Health Composition by function
Summary statistics from NHIS financial statements from NHIA	2005–14	The annual revenues and expenditures of the NHIS, and the state of its investment portfolio
Annual NHIS reports from NHIA	2011–14	Borrowing and interest payments by the NHIA
Annual Ghana Health Service reports	2009, 2011, 2014	Ghana Health Services outpatient visits
Population census data	2010	Population distribution by age groups
NHIS membership data	2014	Demographic information on NHIS members, including age, gender, poverty incidence, membership in the Social Security and National Insurance Trust, etc.
Ghana Demography and Health Survey	2003, 2008, 2014	Self-reported insurance coverage and self-reported knowledge of NHIS features and benefits package
The World Development Indicators	1960–2013	Economic and social development data, including per capita income, life expectancy, the total fertility rate, the maternal mortality rate, the under-five mortality rate, etc.
Payroll data from the Ministry of Health	2016	Information on public workers in health sector by region and focus area
List of health facilities from the Ministry of Health	2016	Health facilities by type and ownership
Volta-specific data		
Claims summary data of Volta region	2014	Information on claims in the Volta region, including service-provider name, NHIS member ID, date of visit, diagnosis, DRG, and cost of treatment (medicine and services)
List of credential facilities in Volta	2014	Information on facilities credentialed as of 2014, including facility name, ownership (public, private, or faith-based), and facility type (primary hospital, secondary hospital, health center, compound, private clinic, etc.)
DRG tariff list	2014	DRG tariffs for each type of facility

are submitted to the Accra Claims Processing Center. Moreover, the findings may serve as baseline information for assessing the impact of capitation in Volta region where the capitation roll-out started in 2015.

The Volta region is reasonably representative of Ghana as a whole, as many of its demographic and development indicators are in the middle of the national spectrum (figure 1.1). At 2.1 million people, Volta's population is close to the median for Ghanaian regions. Volta's poverty rate, urbanization rate, and education indicators are all broadly in line with national averages. The age distribution of NHIS members in Volta is also similar to the national average, and thus their health-risk profile is comparable to that of the population as a whole. Finally, on service provision, Volta is in the middle of the range for the density of public health workers and the degree of private-sector participation in health care.

Figure 1.1 Development Indicators and Health Statistics in the Volta Region

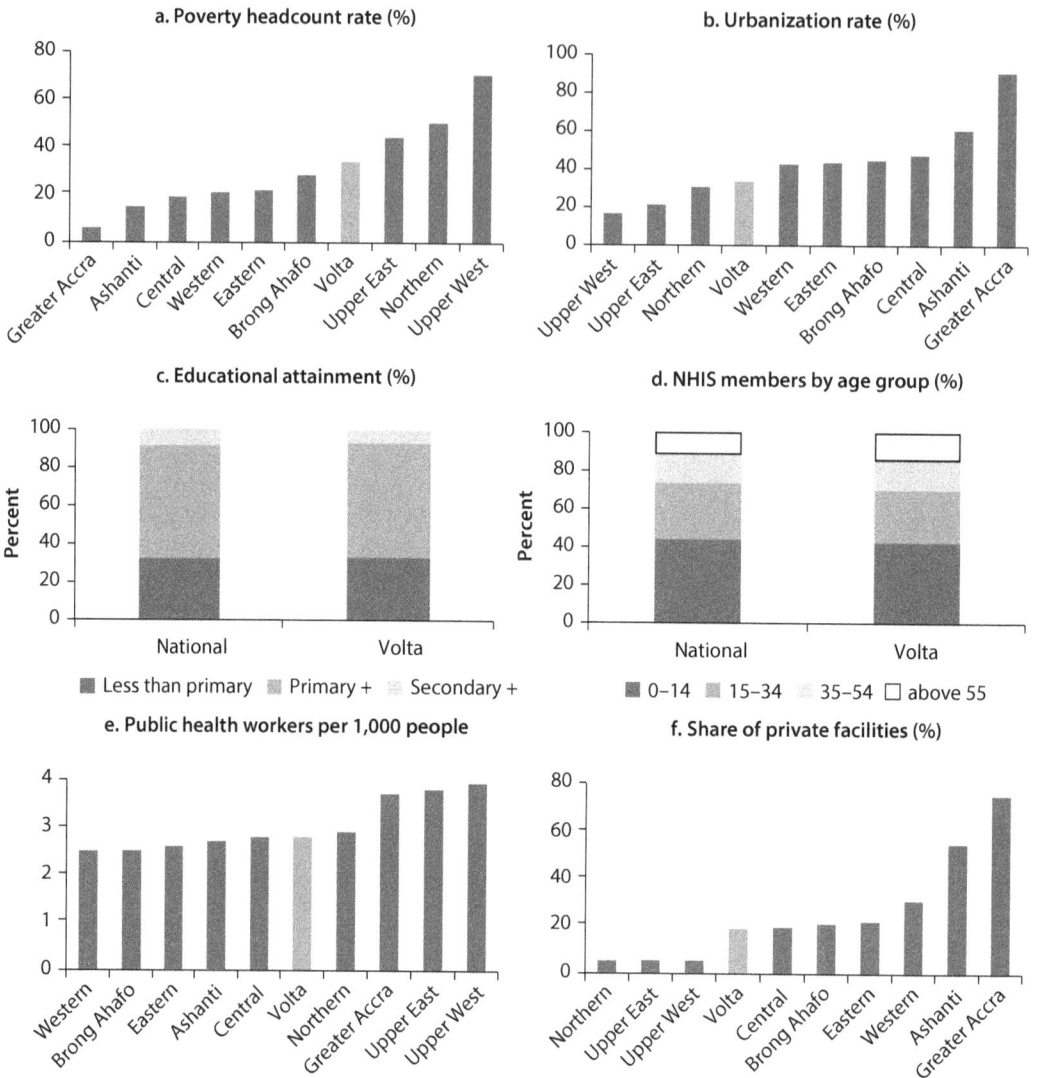

a. Poverty headcount rate (%)

b. Urbanization rate (%)

c. Educational attainment (%)

d. NHIS members by age group (%)

e. Public health workers per 1,000 people

f. Share of private facilities (%)

Sources: GLSS6 for poverty head count; 2010 Population Census for urbanization and education. NHIA membership data for age group distribution; Ministry of Health payroll data for density of public health workers; Ministry of Health inventory of facilities for penetration of private sector.

Despite the Volta region's generally representative characteristics, adjustments will be necessary to apply the results of the Volta-specific analysis to other regions. For example, the Ashanti and Greater Accra regions have many more tertiary hospitals and a larger share of private facilities. This significantly affects the distribution of claims expenditures between facilities of different types, and applying the unadjusted results for the Volta region would underestimate the share of claims expenditures by tertiary hospitals and private facilities.

Organization of the Book

This book comprises six chapters. Following the introduction, chapter 2 provides an overview of the country context and the key features of the health sector. Chapter 3 describes the NHIS, including its revenue structure, expenditure composition, enrollment information, claims-management system, benefits package, provider-payment system, and accreditation services, as well as a summary of its members' knowledge of its essential features. Chapter 4 presents the results of an NHIS claims-expenditure review, which includes historical trends at national level, an overview of claims expenditures in the Volta region, the composition of claims expenditures, and variations among service providers and members. Chapter 5 identifies factors that affect the level and efficiency of NHIS claims expenditures, focusing on behaviors of service providers and patients, as well as NHIA internal management. Chapter 6 concludes with a set of recommendations for designing customized policies for efficient spending in Ghana NHIS.

Notes

1. In a "capitation" system health care providers are paid on a per-patient basis.
2. Ghana's GDP growth rate reached 7.1 percent in 2013, but the inflation rate ended the year at 13.5 percent, up from 8.8 percent in 2012. The fiscal deficit widened to 10.1 percent of GDP, pushing the public debt stock to 56 percent of GDP. Meanwhile, the cedi depreciated against the US dollar by 17.5 percent in 2012 and by 14.6 percent in 2013.
3. Claims data are recorded in Excel files and submitted to NHIA along with paper claims forms.

CHAPTER 2

The Country Context and Key Features of the Ghanaian Health Sector

Country Context

As of 2014, Ghana's total population had reached 26.4 million people, almost 58 percent of whom were below the age of 25. Ghana is divided into 10 administrative regions; the most populous are Ashanti and Greater Accra, while least populous are the Upper West and Upper East. Rural areas are home to just over half of the total population, and the average annual population growth rate is estimated at around 2.5 percent.

Ghana's economy has grown rapidly since the early 2000s. While many countries in Sub-Saharan Africa (SSA) experienced robust expansions during this period, Ghana's GDP growth rate accelerated significantly during the 2000s, reaching an average of 8.7 percent per year between 2008 and 2012. GDP growth outstripped population growth, and the per capita GDP growth rate peaked at 14.5 percent in 2011—the second-highest rate in the world that year. Ghana was upgraded from low-income to lower-middle-income country in 2011.

After successfully narrowing the fiscal deficit by more than three percentage points of GDP in 2015, the government's 2016 budget aims to further reduce the fiscal deficit from 7.1 percent of GDP to 5.3 percent. Ghana's external balances have improved in recent years despite unfavorable global economic conditions. The Ghanaian cedi (GH¢) lost 18 percent of its value against the US dollar in 2015, and the inflation rate rose from 17.7 percent in February 2015 to 18.5 percent in February 2016. The GDP growth rate slowed for the fourth consecutive year, falling from 4 percent in 2014 to an estimated 3.4 percent in 2015, as energy rationing, high inflation, and an ongoing process of fiscal consolidation inhibited economic activity.

Although Ghana achieved its Millennium Development Goal of halving the poverty rate, a large share of the population remains below poverty line. The poverty rate dropped from 52 percent in 1991 to 21 percent in 2012,[1] but 6.4 million Ghanaians continue to live below the poverty line. Poverty rates vary substantially by region, ranging from 71 percent in the Upper West region to less than 6 percent in the Accra region.

Health Outcomes

Ghana's key health indicators improved steadily over the past several decades. In 2013, average life expectancy at birth was 61 years, the maternal mortality rate (MMR) was 321 deaths per 100,000 live births, the total fertility rate (TFR) was 3.9 births per woman, and the under-five mortality (U5M) rate was 67 deaths per 1,000 live births. Moreover, Ghana outperformed the SSA average on each of these indicators (table 2.1). However, the country's strong overall performance masks significant disparities between income groups (figure 2.1).

Table 2.1 Health Outcome Indicators in Ghana, 1960–2013

	Ghana							SSA[a]
	1960	1970	1980	1990	2000	2010	2013	2013
Life expectancy	46	49	52	57	57	61	61	58
Maternal mortality ratio	N/A	N/A	N/A	634	467	325	321	573
Total fertility rate	6.7	7	6.5	5.6	4.7	4.1	3.9	5.0
Under-five mortality	211	202	166	127	101	75	67	89

Source: World Development Indicators Database.
Note: N/A = not available.
a. SSA countries developing only.

Figure 2.1 Equity in Health Outcomes, 2003–14

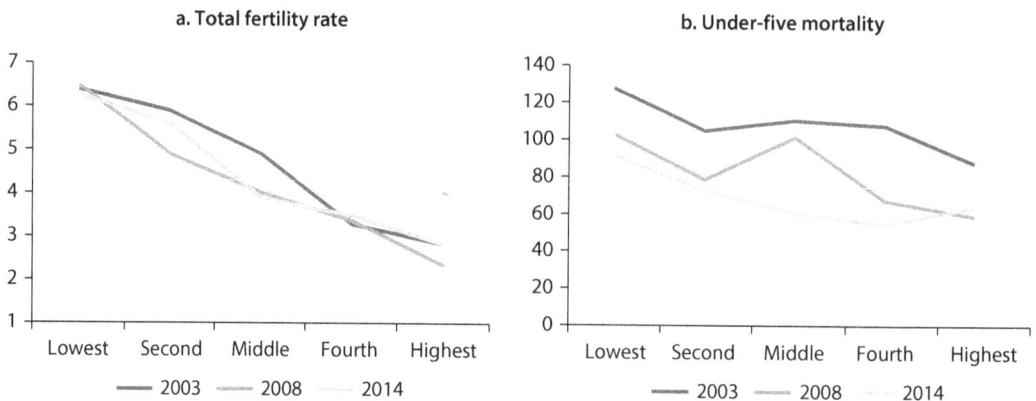

a. Total fertility rate

b. Under-five mortality

——— 2003 ——— 2008 ——— 2014

Source: Ghana DHSs 2003, 2008, and 2014.

Figure 2.2 Ghana's Global Rank on Key Economic and Health Indicators, 1990–2013

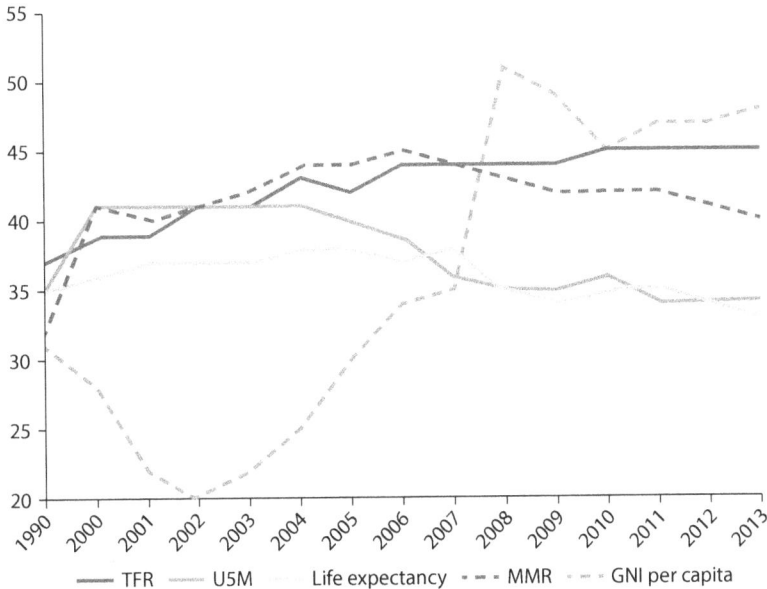

Source: World Development Indicators Database.
Note: Ranks begin at 1; higher scores indicate improvement relative to other countries.

Over the past decade, Ghana's health indicators have failed to keep pace with its economic indicators. Ghana's global ranking in per capita GNI rose from 20th in 2002 to 49th in 2013, but its global ranking in major health indicators such as life expectancy, MMR and U5M peaked between 2005 and 2007 and then declined, with life expectancy and U5M falling back to their 1990 level by 2013. Since 2008, Ghana's global rank for GNI per capita has exceeded its rank for all major health indicators (figure 2.2).

Health Services

Service Utilization
The government's efforts to expand the coverage of health services have yielded mixed results. The share of births attended by a skilled health care worker has increased significantly, rising from 47.1 percent in 2003 to 73.7 percent in 2014. However, the coverage rate of modern contraceptives rose only slightly from 18.7 percent in 2003 to 22.2 percent in 2014. Meanwhile, immunization coverage declined between 2008 and 2014, and the share of children with fever taking antimalarial medication was far lower in 2014 than in 2003, before the establishment of the National Health Insurance Scheme (NHIS) (see table 2.2). The number of outpatient visits increased sharply from 0.5 per capita during 2001–06 to 1.1 per capita during 2011–14.

Table 2.2 Coverage of Essential Services, 2003–14 (%)

	2003	2008	2014
Children fully immunized	69.4	79.0	77.3
Taking anti-malaria drug among children with fever	62.8	43.0	48.5
Skilled birth attendance	47.1	58.7	73.7
Use of modern contraceptives	18.7	16.6	22.2

Source: Ghana DHSs 2003, 2008 and 2014.

Figure 2.3 Coverage of Essential Services, by Wealth Quintiles, 2003–14

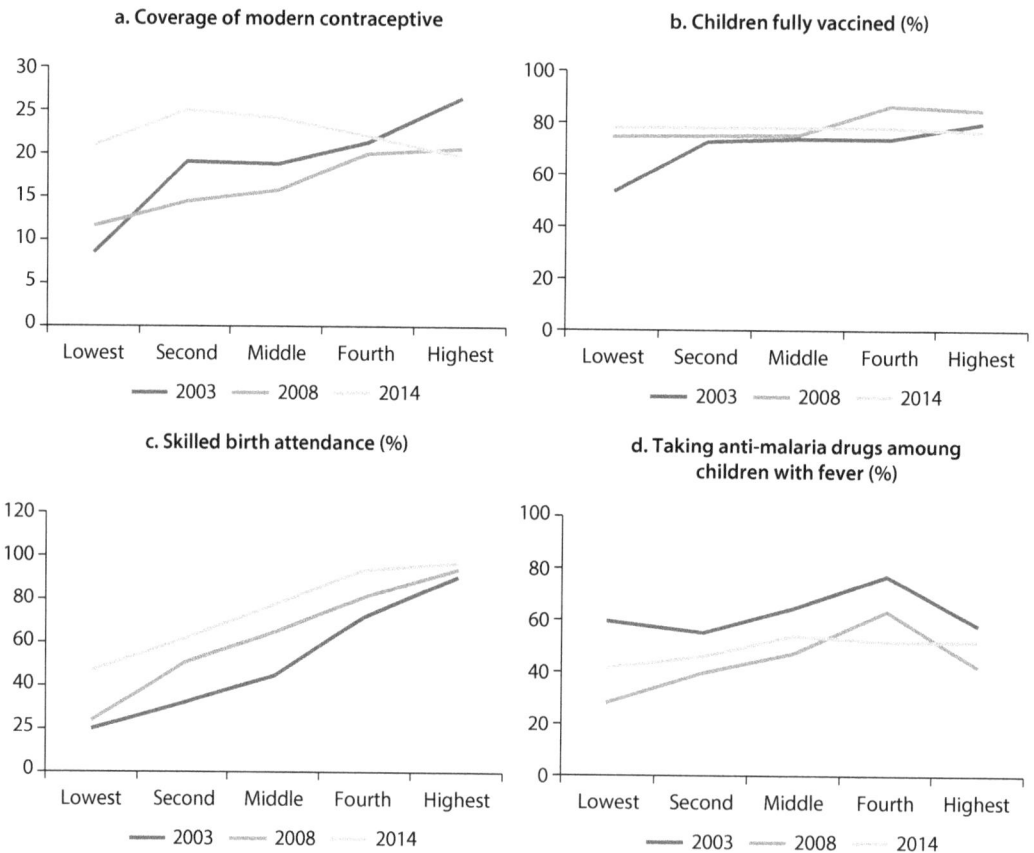

Source: Ghana DHSs 2003, 2008 and 2014.

Equity in Service Access

Despite improvements in some indicators, utilization rates for health services are far from equal across income groups. Coverage rates for modern contraceptives, vaccinations and malaria treatments are relatively equitable, though rates for modern contraceptives and malaria treatment are low for all income groups (figure 2.3). The greatest disparity is in the share of births attended by a skilled health care worker; the coverage rate in highest quintile (96.7 percent) is more than double that of lowest quintile (46.9 percent).

Health Service Delivery System

Health Facilities

There are an estimated 3,500 public, private, and faith-based health care facilities in Ghana. Fifty-seven percent of these facilities are public, 33 percent are private, and 7 percent are operated by the Christian Health Association of Ghana (CHAG) (figure 2.4). Health facilities include compounds, health centers, clinics, maternity homes, and seven types of hospitals: district, municipal, metropolitan, regional, teaching, psychiatric and uncategorized (table 2.3). While all compounds and most health centers and district hospitals are public, most clinics, maternity

Figure 2.4 Health Care Facilities, by Ownership

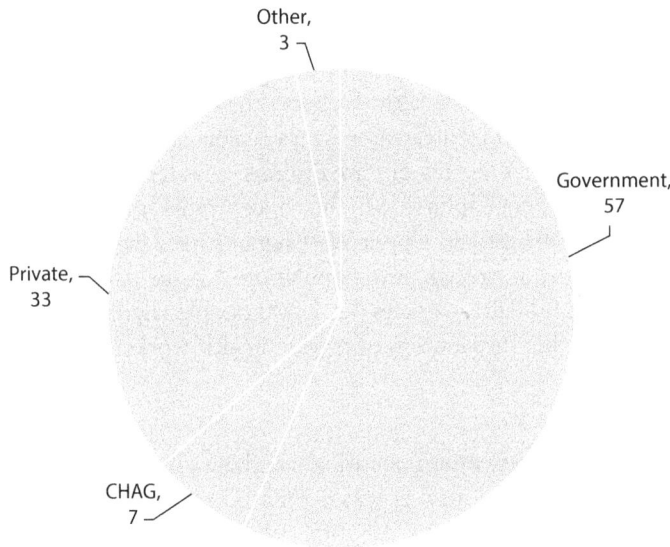

Table 2.3 Health Care Facilities, by Type

Facility type	Number
CHPS	653
Clinic	1,173
Health center	787
Maternity home	369
Polyclinic	16
District hospital	82
Hospital (unidentified)	276
Metropolitan/municipal hospital	5
Regional hospital	9
Psychiatric hospital	3
Teaching hospital	3
Others	183

Source: Health facilities inventory list, Ministry of Health.

homes, and uncategorized hospitals are private. One municipal hospital is CHAG-owned, and one teaching hospital is private; all other municipal, metropolitan, regional, and teaching hospitals are public facilities. The share of private facilities ranges from 5.4 percent in the Northern region to 74.9 percent in the Greater Accra region.

Human Resources

As of February 2016, an estimated 104,652 health care workers were employed by public and CHAG facilities, with nurses comprising the bulk of the workforce.[2] No employment data are available for private facilities. Eighty-four percent of workers in public and CHAG facilities are health care professionals, 15 percent are administrative officials, and 1 percent are logistics specialists. Most health professionals are nurses (59 percent), followed by trainees (13 percent), allied health professionals (13 percent), physician assistants (4 percent), and doctors (4 percent).

The distribution of public health workers is broadly consistent across regions, though the heavily urbanized Greater Accra region and the sparsely populated Upper East and Upper West regions are outliers. Greater Accra has a high number of health workers per capita due to the concentration of doctors in the capital city, while the Upper East and Upper West regions have high numbers of health workers per capita due to their low population density. All other regions have between 2.5 and 2.9 health workers per 1,000 people (figure 2.5). No information is available on the distribution of private health workers.

Pharmaceuticals

Ghana has an enormous pharmaceutical market. The value of the country's wholesale pharmaceutical market was estimated at US$522 million in 2014.[3] Imports comprise 60 percent of total pharmaceuticals by volume and

Figure 2.5 Number of Health Workers per 1,000 People, by Region, 2016

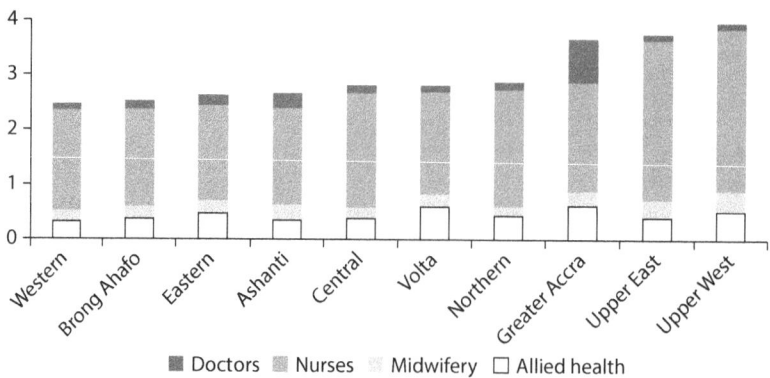

Source: Payroll data, Ministry of Health.

70–80 percent by value, as most domestic manufactures can only produce low-cost generic drugs. Its dependence on imported pharmaceuticals exposes NHIS to price changes and exchange-rate volatility.

The private sector dominates pharmaceutical distribution. The MoH procurement unit has an annual budget of about US$40 million, of which US$35 million is provided by development partners. Centrally procured medicines are limited to antiretroviral drugs, antimalarial drugs, oxytocin, snake antivenin, rabies vaccine, and a few other special items. An estimated 80 percent of pharmaceutics dispensed in public health facilities are procured by regions or facilities directly from private distributors.

Health Financing System

Ghana's health sector is mainly financed by the government, its development partners, and Ghanaian households. Public resources are allocated to the Ministry of Health (MoH) and health facilities through budgetary transfers, while the National Health Insurance Authority (NHIA) is funded by the national health insurance (NHI) levy and by Social Security and National Insurance Trust (SSNIT) deductions. Ghana's development partners also support the MoH, NHIA, and individual health facilities through grants, technical assistance, and concessional and commercial loans. Household contributions include NHIS premium payments and out-of-pocket spending at the point of care (figure 2.6).

Figure 2.6 The Flow of Funds in the Ghanaian Health Sector

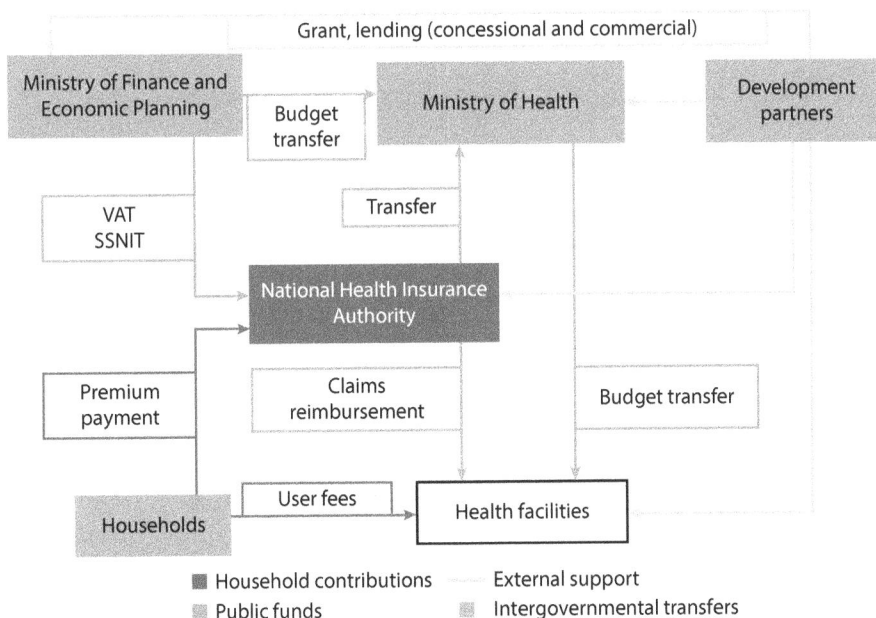

Per capita health spending has increased over the past decade, and the sources of funding have shifted away from donors and towards the government and households. Nominal per capita health spending rose from GH¢29 in 2005 to GH¢140 in 2012, and spending increased in real terms as well (figure 2.7). In 2005, Ghana's development partners financed more than half of the country's total health expenditures. As the NHIS expanded, the government's share increased significantly, and in 2010 public funding accounted for more than two-thirds of health spending. However, from 2010 to 2012 the share of private funds—mostly out-of-pocket payments—almost tripled, while both public funds and external assistance declined (figures 2.7 and 2.8).

Figure 2.7 Per Capita Total Health Spending, 2005–12

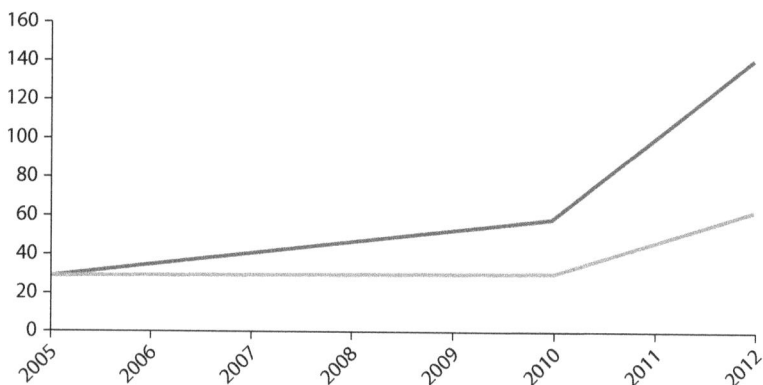

Source: Ghana National Health Account Study 2005, 2010, and 2012.

Figure 2.8 Financing Sources of Total Health Expenditure, 2005–12

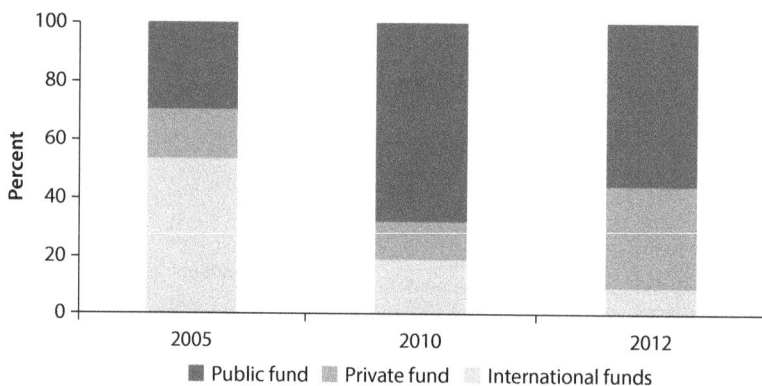

Source: Ghana National Health Account Study 2005, 2010, and 2012.

Notes

1. For the sake of comparability, the 2012 poverty headcount was calculated using the 1999 poverty line. Under the 2012 poverty line, the poverty rate would be 24.2 percent. See World Bank (2015b).

2. This estimate is based on consolidated payroll data.

3. IMS Health (2015), "African Insights—Ghana."

CHAPTER 3

NHIS Overview

Basic Features

Revenues and Expenditures

The National Health Insurance Scheme (NHIS) is financed primarily by tax revenue, and claims make up the bulk of its expenditures. The NHI levy provides 74 percent of NHIS revenue, Social Security and National Insurance Trust (SSNIT) deductions comprise another 20 percent, and premium payments provide just 3 percent. Meanwhile, claims payments account for 77 percent of NHIS expenditures (figure 3.1). Due to the low level of MoH spending on goods and services, NHIS claims payments represent over 80 percent of health facilities' operational expenses (figure 3.2).[1]

Ghana is the only country in the world to finance its health insurance scheme primarily through value-added tax (VAT) revenue. This ensures that NHIS revenue automatically keeps pace with economic growth, as is underscored by the stability of NHIS revenue as a share of total government spending. Using the VAT to finance health care also creates an implicit subsidy for basic care, and it provides a basis for pooling risks and costs at the national level, which prevents the scheme fragmentation experienced by many other countries. However, this mechanism has one major disadvantage, which is revenue does not increase as coverage expands.

Member Enrollment

All residents of Ghana, including non-citizens, are eligible for NHIS coverage, but not all enrollees are required to pay premiums. SSNIT contributors do not pay premiums, nor do enrollees under the age of 18 or over the age of 70. Indigent people, institutionalized people and beneficiaries of social protection programs may also be exempted from premium payments.

Over time, NHIS enrollment has expanded and become more equitable. As of 2014, the NHIS covered about 40 percent of the population. More than

Figure 3.1 NHIS Revenue Composition, 2005–14
percent

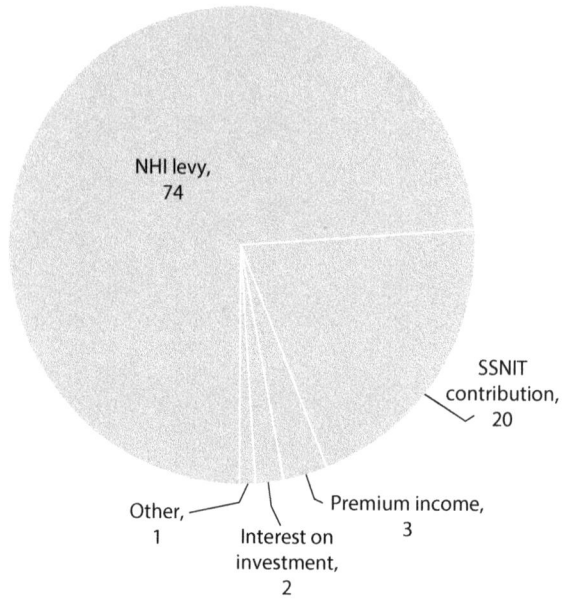

NHI levy,
74

SSNIT
contribution,
20

Premium income,
3

Interest on
investment,
2

Other,
1

Source: Summary statistics from NHIS financial statements from NHIA.

Figure 3.2 NHIS Expenditure Composition, 2014
percent

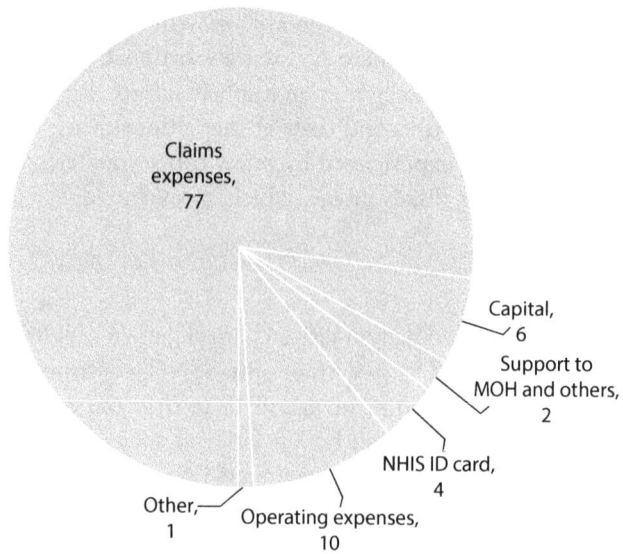

Claims
expenses,
77

Capital,
6

Support to
MOH and others,
2

NHIS ID card,
4

Operating expenses,
10

Other,
1

Source: Summary statistics from NHIS financial statements from NHIA.

Figure 3.3 NHIS Membership Composition, 2014
percent

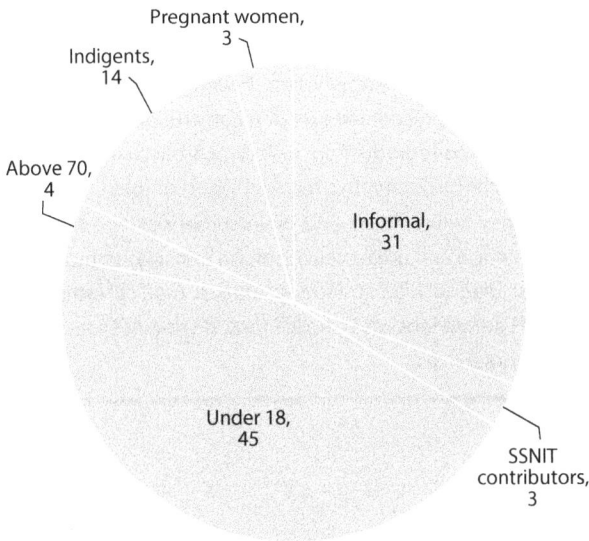

Pregnant women, 3

Indigents, 14

Above 70, 4

Informal, 31

Under 18, 45

SSNIT contributors, 3

Source: NHIA annual reports.

Figure 3.4 NHIS Coverage, by Wealth Quintiles, 2008–14

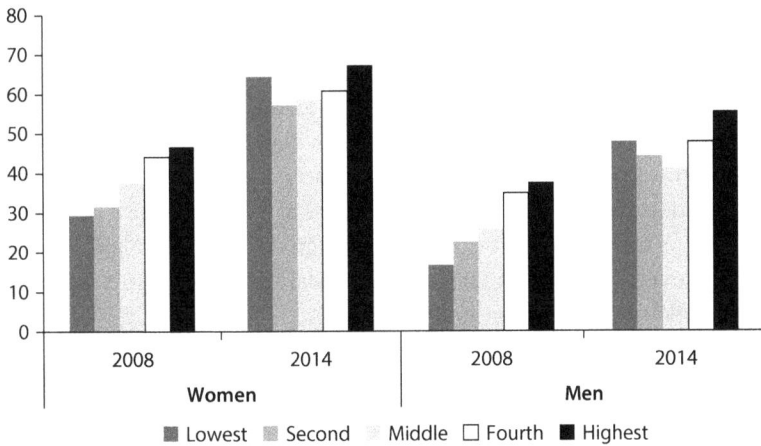

■ Lowest ■ Second Middle □ Fourth ■ Highest

Source: Ghana DHSs 2008 and 2014.

two-thirds of NHIS members are exempted from premium payments (figure 3.3). The indigents group accounts for 14 percent of all NHIS members. Moreover, NHIS coverage has also become more equitable from 2008 to 2014 (figure 3.4); the ratio between the highest and lowest quintile among women decreased from 1.6 to 1.0.

Box 3.1 NHIS Exclusions

The following health care services are not covered by the NHIS:
Rehabilitation other than physiotherapy; vision, hearing, orthopedic and dental aids and prostheses; elective cosmetic procedures except reconstructive surgery; antiretroviral drugs for treating HIV/AIDS; assisted reproduction, including artificial insemination and hormone-replacement therapy; echocardiography; medical photography; angiography; orthoptics; dialysis for chronic kidney failure; heart and brain surgery except to repair trauma; cancer treatment other than cervical and breast cancer; organ transplants; medicines not included in the NHIS Medicines List; diagnosis and treatment abroad; medical examinations for purposes of employment, school admissions, visa applications, driving licenses, etc.; VIP ward accommodation; and mortuary services.

Benefits Package

NHIS covers 95 percent of diagnosed conditions, and it has no cost-sharing requirements. NHIS policy covers all outpatient, inpatient, and emergency care, and a list of excluded conditions is explicitly defined (box 3.1). NHIS members pay no out-of-pocket costs for services or pharmaceuticals based on policy.

Claims Management

Claims management is a vital component of NHIS operations. On average, National Health Insurance Authority (NHIA) processes 2.4 million claims each month.[2] Most claims are submitted via paper forms; only 8 percent are submitted electronically. Once providers submit their claims, the NHIA subjects them to a 5-step process: fulfillment, vetting, data entry, vetting-report generation, and payment request initiation (figure 3.5). A typical vetting report includes information on the total amount deducted for a given batch of claims from each facility. However, some providers have complained that these reports do not include specific information on individual claims.

Provider Payments

Under the NHIS, providers were initially paid only on a fee-for-service (FFS) basis, but over time the payment system evolved to encompass Ghana diagnosis-related-groups (GDRG) and capitation. As FFS payments can incentivize an oversupply of services, GDRG and capitation payments were introduced to contain costs. While capitation payments are used for outpatient primary care in some regions of Ghana, GDRG are used for all inpatient care, all outpatient care in non-capitation regions, and outpatient specialty care in capitation regions. Pharmaceutical costs are still reimbursed to providers on an FFS basis, which reflects predetermined tariffs and quantities of drugs submitted by providers.

Figure 3.5 NHIA Claims-Processing Flowchart

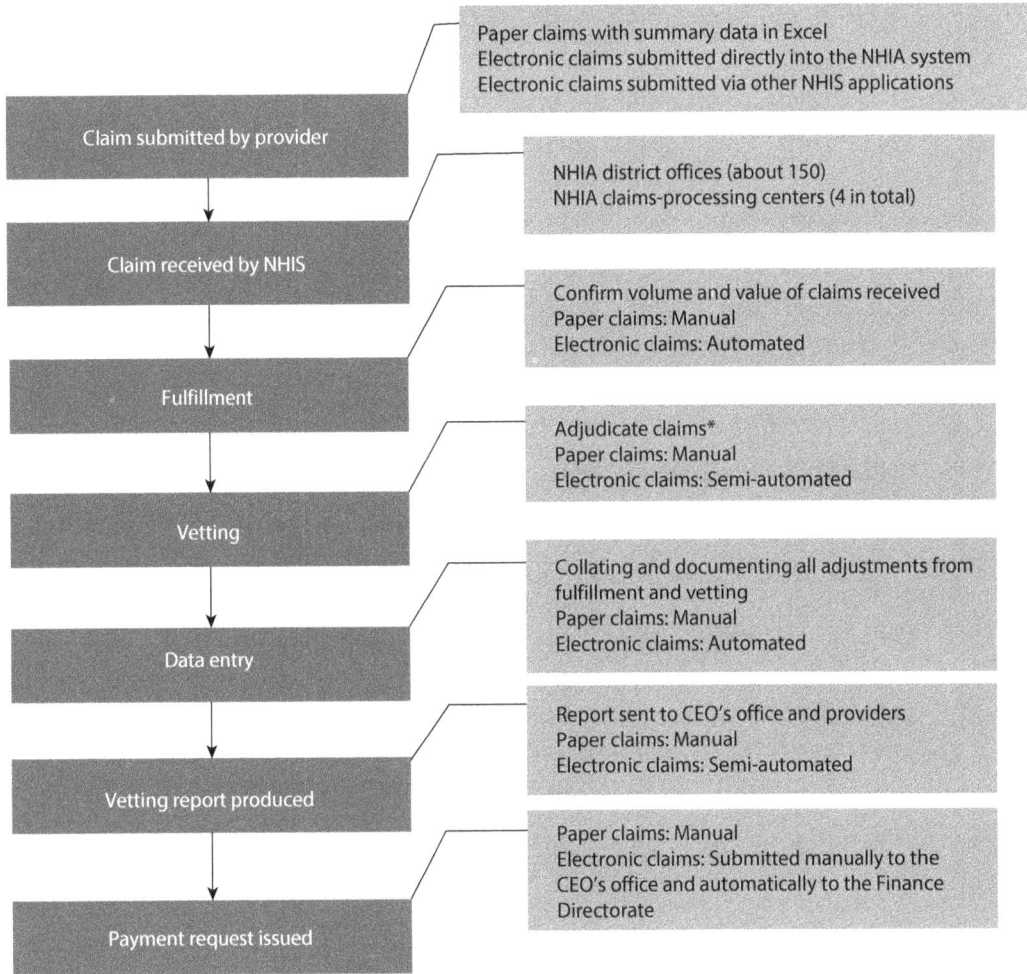

Claim submitted by provider	Paper claims with summary data in Excel Electronic claims submitted directly into the NHIA system Electronic claims submitted via other NHIS applications
↓	
Claim received by NHIS	NHIA district offices (about 150) NHIA claims-processing centers (4 in total)
↓	
Fulfillment	Confirm volume and value of claims received Paper claims: Manual Electronic claims: Automated
↓	
Vetting	Adjudicate claims* Paper claims: Manual Electronic claims: Semi-automated
↓	
Data entry	Collating and documenting all adjustments from fulfillment and vetting Paper claims: Manual Electronic claims: Automated
↓	
Vetting report produced	Report sent to CEO's office and providers Paper claims: Manual Electronic claims: Semi-automated
↓	
Payment request issued	Paper claims: Manual Electronic claims: Submitted manually to the CEO's office and automatically to the Finance Directorate

Private health care providers receive higher GDRG tariffs and capitation rates to compensate for their lack of public funding. Public providers (including Christian Health Association of Ghana [CHAG] facilities) receive funding from the MoH, whereas private providers do not receive it. Consequently, tariff rates differ significantly by facility type and ownership. For example, the reimbursable cost of a general consultation for an adult patient is 76 percent higher for a private primary hospital and 48 percent higher for a private clinic than it is for a public primary hospital (table 3.1).

Provider Accreditation
Health facilities require NHIA accreditation to provide services to NHIS members. Once an application is received, along with the required

Table 3.1 Tariff Rates for Selected DRGs, by Facility Type (GH¢)

	Public primary hospital	CHAG primary hospital	Private primary hospital	Private clinic
OPDC6A (general consultation, adults)	8.91	10.13	10.13	13.17
OPDC6C (general consultation, children)	8.72	9.79	9.79	11.98
MEDI28A (malaria treatment, adults)	37.63	38.95	38.95	N/A
PAED36C (malaria treatment, children)	36.34	37.61	37.61	N/A

Source: NHIA 2014.
Note: N/A = not applicable.

Box 3.2 NHIA Accreditation Criteria

A facility that wishes to apply for NHIA accreditation must:

- Have already received accreditation from a national regulatory body: Ghana Health Services, the Health Professional Regulatory Authority, or the Pharmacy Council.
- Have been in operation for at least six months prior to the application.
- Be in good standing for service provision.
- Provide information on staff levels, physical infrastructure, and services provided.
- Accept the NHIA's quality-assurance standards and payment mechanisms.
- Agree to allow on-site inspections by the NHIA or its authorized representatives and implement corrective measures as necessary.

---

documentation and fees, the NHIA verifies that the submitted documents are complete and then sends an accreditation toolkit to the facility. The NHIA's quality-assurance department undertakes a detailed assessment of the facility and submits a report to NHIA management, which makes the final decision. Box 3.2 presents NHIA accrediation criteria.

Member Knowledge about the Basic Features of the NHIS

Survey data show that NHIS members have limited knowledge of the benefits to which they are entitled. About half of NHIS members are aware that enrollees under the age of 18 are exempt from paying premiums; about 70 percent know that pregnant women are exempt; and about 60 percent know that NHIS members are not required to make out-of-pocket payments. However, only 29 percent of NHIS members are aware of all three features (figure 3.6). A similar patterns is observed for benefit packages: although 60–70 percent of members are aware of each individual service (antenatal care, postnatal care, childbirth and cash transfers), only 39 percent are aware of all five (figure 3.7).

Figure 3.6 Knowledge of NHIS Enrollment Features among NHIS Members

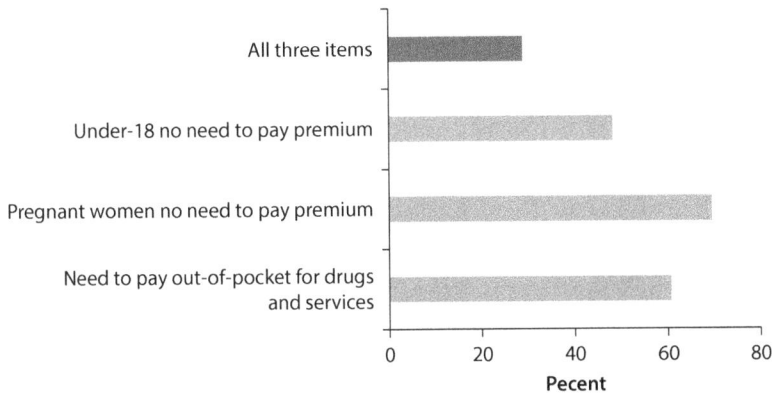

Source: Ghana DHS 2014.

Figure 3.7 Knowledge of NHIS Benefits among NHIS Members

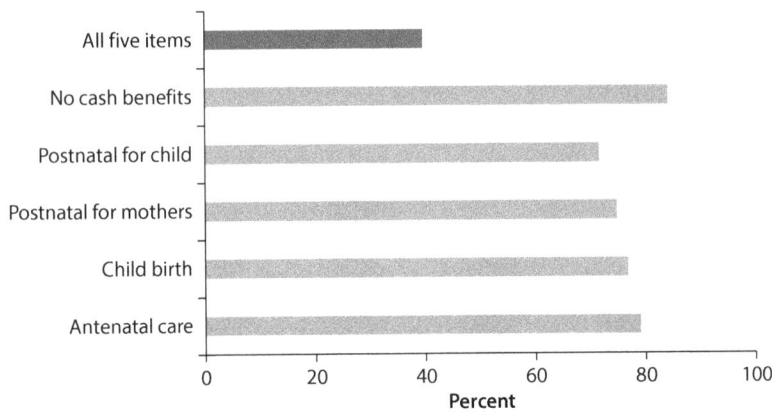

Source: Ghana DHS 2014.

NHIS's Role in Health Care Financing

The National Health Insurance Fund is the second-largest component of public health spending. VAT revenue and SSNIT deductions finance the fund. In 2014, it provided about Ghanaian cedi (GH¢) 1.6 billion to the Ministry of Health, GH¢0.9 billion to the National Health Fund, GH¢3.3 million for capital investment, and GH¢0.5 billion for health-sector projects financed by external loans (figure 3.8).

Since 2012, the NHIS has played an increasing important role in public health financing. The National Health Fund has always represented about 3 percent of total public spending. However, the share of MoH expenditures rose to a peak of 8.5 percent of total public spending in 2012, then fell to 5 percent in 2014, the same share as in 2010 (figure 3.9).

Figure 3.8 Public Health Financing, by Mechanism, 2014

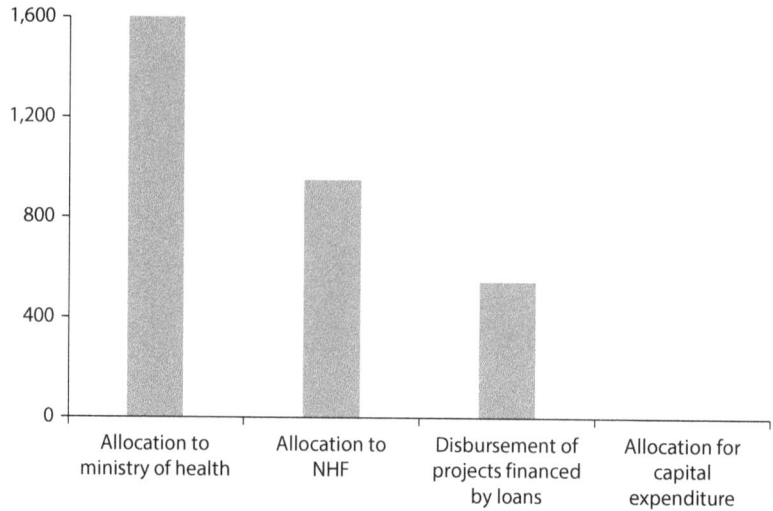

Source: Holistic assessment of the health sector program of 2014, MoH.

Figure 3.9 Spending on MoH and NHIS as a Share of Total Public Spending, 2010–14

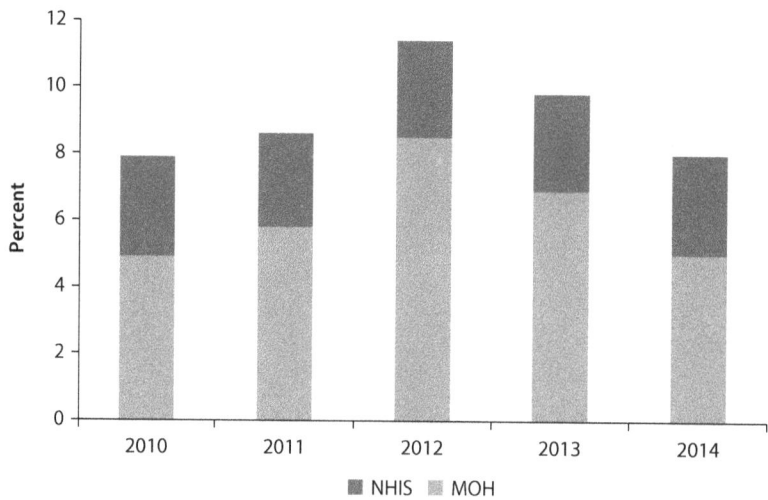

Source: Ghana consolidated accounts and fiscal accounts.

The NHIS is a major source of operational financing for health facilities. Funds allocated to the MoH cover more than 95 percent of personnel compensation but a negligible share of non-salary recurrent expenditures for frontline health care workers. Consequently, health facilities must rely on NHIS reimbursement to recover their operational expenses.[3] Total public spending on goods and services for the MoH, Ghana Health Services and CHAG reached about GH¢140 million in 2014 (figure 3.10).

Figure 3.10 Public Spending on Goods and Services, by Recipient, 2012–15

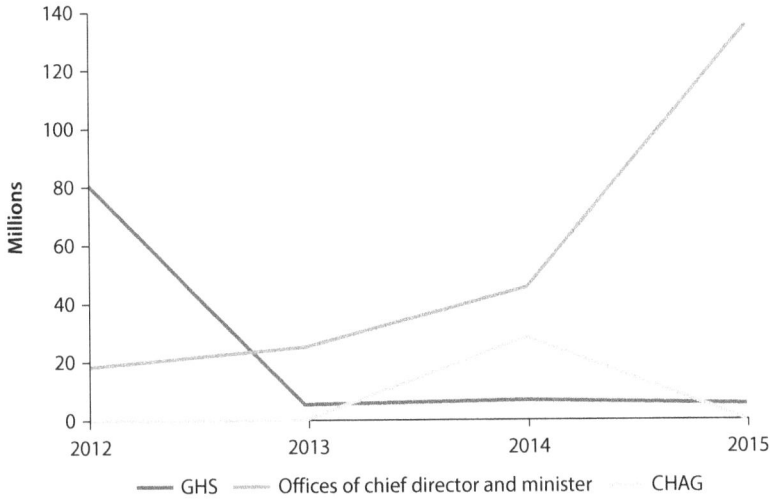

Source: Ghana consolidated accounts.
Note: Data for year 2015 is budget data, not actual expenditure data.

Notes

1. Based on interviews with key informants in MoH.

2. This information comes from a 2015 NHIA presentation.

3. The other source of operational expenses for health facilities is out-of-pocket payments, represent about 20 percent of operational expenses according to interviews with MoH officials.

CHAPTER 4

NHIS Claims–Expenditure Review

Trends in NHIS Claims Expenditures over Time

The growth of claims expenditures has outpaced the growth of National Health Insurance Scheme (NHIS) revenue since 2009, causing a sizable deficit. Claims expenditures rose from Ghanaian cedi (GH¢) 7.6 million in 2005 to GH¢1.1 billion in 2014. In 2008, the NHIS had a surplus of GH¢492 million, but in 2009 it began running a deficit each year. By 2014, this deficit had widened to GH¢300 million (figure 4.1). The deficit disrupts NHIS operations including its reimbursement schedule, and the situation gets worse when NHI levy contributions are not released on time.

Several factors have contributed to the increase in claims expenditures over time. Total claims expenditures are determined by insurance coverage, service utilization, and average unit costs.[1] Rising NHIS claims expenditures were driven by an increase in utilization (i.e., the number of claims per member) from 2005 to 2008, an expansion of coverage (i.e., the number of members) from 2008 to 2011, and rising unit costs (i.e., the average cost per claim) from 2011 to 2014 (see table 4.1).

The NHIS has been drawing down its investment fund to finance its deficit. The NHIS investment fund has been declining since 2009, when the system began running a regular annual deficit (figure 4.2). The investment fund fell from GH¢447 million (or 14.8 months of claims value) in 2009 to 100.3 million (or 1.2 months of claims value) in 2014. However, withdrawals from the investment fund have been insufficient to cover the deficit since 2012.

The National Health Insurance Authority (NHIA) has contracted loans to finance the deficit. According to its annual reports, the NHIA took out a loan of over GH¢100 million in 2011 and began paying interest on it in 2012. The outstanding balance peaked at GH¢140 million in 2012, and interest payments reached almost GH¢40 million in 2013 (figure 4.3).

Figure 4.1 NHIS Revenues and Expenditures, 2005–14 (GH¢ millions)

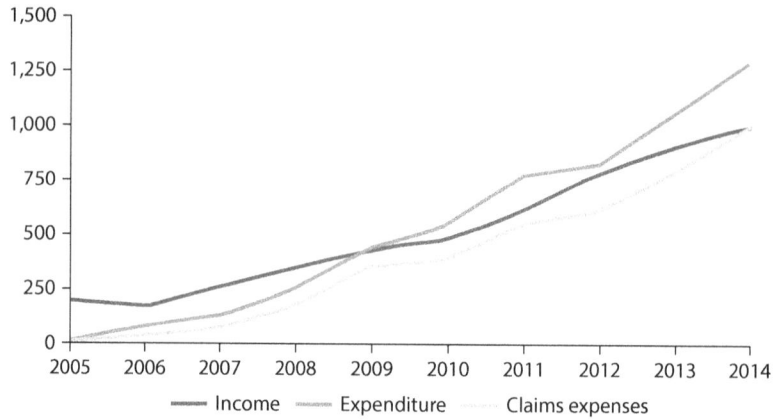

Source: Summary statistics from NHIS financial statements from NHIA.

Table 4.1 Changes in the Total Claims Expenditures, by Component
Percent

	Total claims payments	Total number of members	Number of claims per member	Average cost per claim
2005–08	2308.0	154.8	524.1[a]	51.4
2008–11	199.8	139.2[a]	13.0	10.9
2011–12	12.3	8.0	−13.0	19.6[a]
2012–13	27.8	9.8	4.3	11.6[a]
2013–14	36.4	7.6	0.3	26.4[a]

Source: Ghana NHIA annual reports.
a. Values represent the major drivers of NHIS claims expenditures.

Figure 4.2 NHIS Balance and Changes in Investment Fund Assets (GH¢ millions)

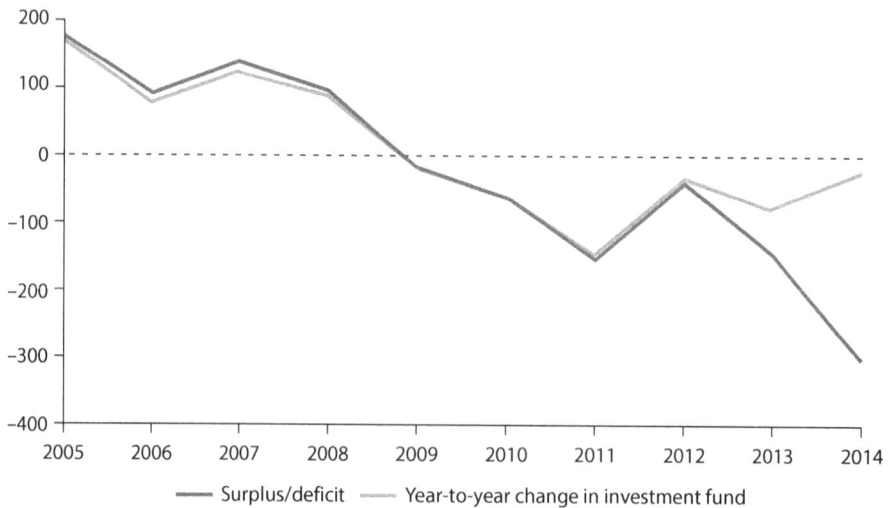

Source: Ghana NHIS annual reports.

Figure 4.3 NHIS Loan Balance and Interest Payments (GH¢ millions)

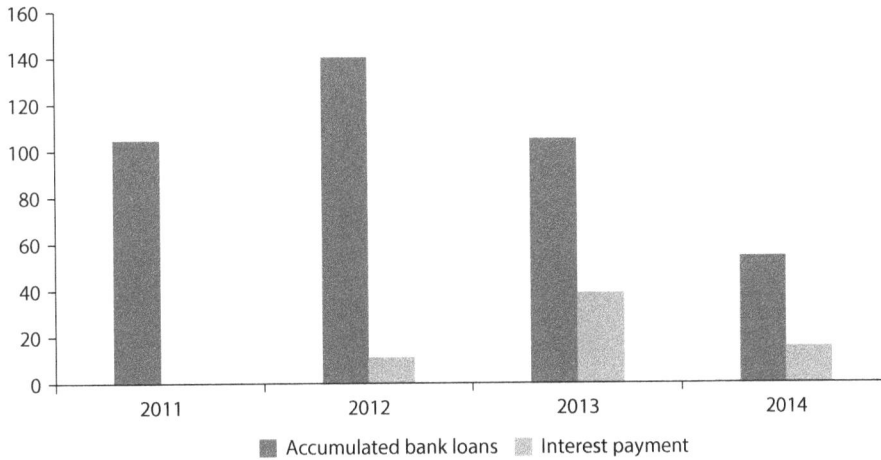

Accumulated bank loans ■ Interest payment

Source: Ghana NHIS annual reports.

Overview of Claims Expenditures in the Volta Region

Health care providers in the Volta region claimed GH¢68 million in NHIA reimbursements during 2014. The data used for this study cover an estimated 95 percent of all claims. The analysis focuses on claims with clean data, meaning those that have valid NHIS identification numbers and diagnosis-related-group (DRG) codes and are submitted by NHIA-accredited providers. These claims amount to GH¢56.6 million, or 82 percent of total claims expenditures. Chapter 5 examines in greater detail the small share of claims excluded from the chapter's analysis.

Outpatient services is the main component of claims expenditure. In 2014, outpatient claims represented 72 percent of claims expenditures in Volta, while inpatient claims represented just 28 percent (figure 4.4). Within outpatient claims, medicine accounts for a larger share relative to medical services (38 vs. 34 percent of total claims expenditure). By contrast, medicine accounts for a small share of inpatient claims relative to service costs (8 vs. 20 percent of total claims expenditure). Ninety-six percent of claims include medicine as an expenditure.

Five groups of Ghana diagnosis-related-groups (GDRGs) account for 80 percent of all claims expenditures in Volta. The most common diagnosis group is general outpatient consultation, which accounts for more than half of all claims costs. Roughly half of all outpatient consultations are malaria-related. Along with outpatient consultations, GDRGs for conditions related to childbirth, infection, and hypertension are the largest contributors to claims expenditures, representing 24 percent in total (figure 4.5). This distribution pattern is consistent across different facility levels and ownership types.

Figure 4.4 Claims Expenditures, by Service Type, Volta, 2014
percent

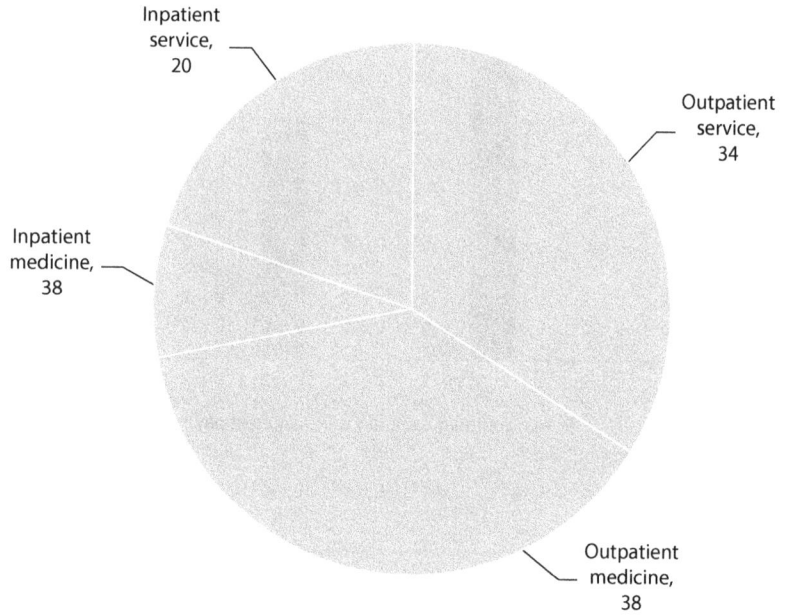

Inpatient service, 20

Outpatient service, 34

Inpatient medicine, 38

Outpatient medicine, 38

Source: Ghana NHIS claims expenditure in Volta region.

Figure 4.5 Claims Expenditures, by GDRG, Volta, 2014
percent

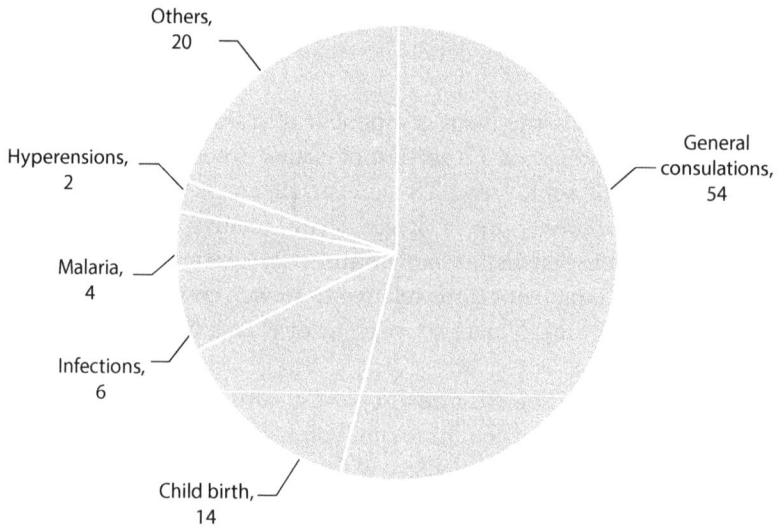

Others, 20

General consulations, 54

Hyperensions, 2

Malaria, 4

Infections, 6

Child birth, 14

Source: Ghana NHIS claims expenditure in Volta region.

Claims Expenditure Distribution and Variation, by Provider

Primary hospitals and public facilities account for the largest share of claims by total value. Fifty-seven percent of outpatient and 90 percent of inpatient claims expenditures are incurred at primary hospitals. Secondary hospital (i.e., Volta regional hospital) accounts for just 3.7 percent of outpatient and 8.3 of inpatient claims, but this share may be larger in regions with more sophisticated secondary and tertiary hospitals. Health centers and private clinics are also major providers of outpatient services, accounting for 21 and 14 percent of outpatient claims expenditures in Volta (figure 4.6). Public facilities account for 53 percent of both outpatient and inpatient claims expenditures; faith-based facilities account for 35 percent of inpatient claims and 23 percent of outpatient claims; and private facilities account for 24 percent of outpatient claims and 10 percent of inpatient claims (figure 4.7).

Figure 4.6 Distribution of Claims Expenditures, by Facility Type, Volta, 2014

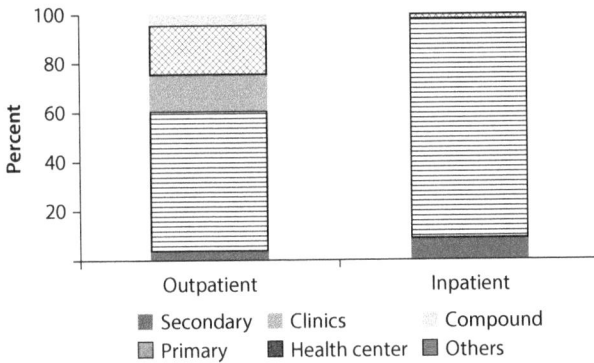

Source: Ghana NHIS claims expenditure in Volta region.

Figure 4.7 Distribution of Claims Expenditures, by Facility Ownership, Volta, 2014

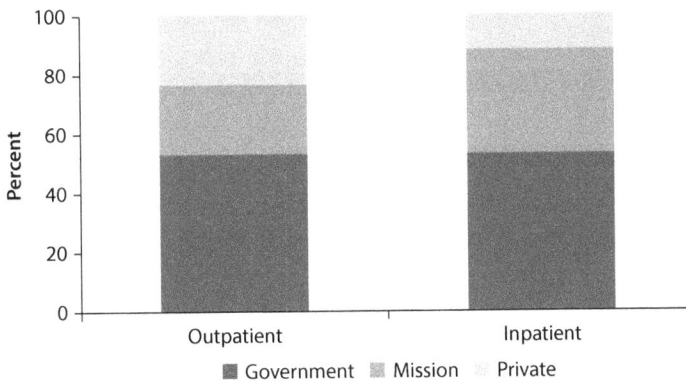

Source: Ghana NHIS claims expenditure in Volta region.

Average per-claim expenditures tends to be higher in hospitals and in non-public facilities. Among public facilities, per-claim expenditures for outpatient services are much lower in compounds and health centers (GH¢8.8 and GH¢9.9, respectively) than in primary hospitals (GH¢22.8) and secondary hospitals (GH¢22.0). The same pattern is observed among non-public facilities: per-claim expenditures are 28 percent higher at faith-based primary hospitals than at faith-based health centers and 102 percent higher at private hospitals than at private health centers (figure 4.8). Per-claim expenditures for inpatient services are 35 percent higher at private hospitals than at public hospitals. Per-claim expenditures at private clinics are also significantly higher than at public hospitals, due largely to the higher reimbursement rates for non-public facilities figure 4.9).

Figure 4.8 Per-Claim Expenditures, by Facility Type and Ownership, Outpatient Services

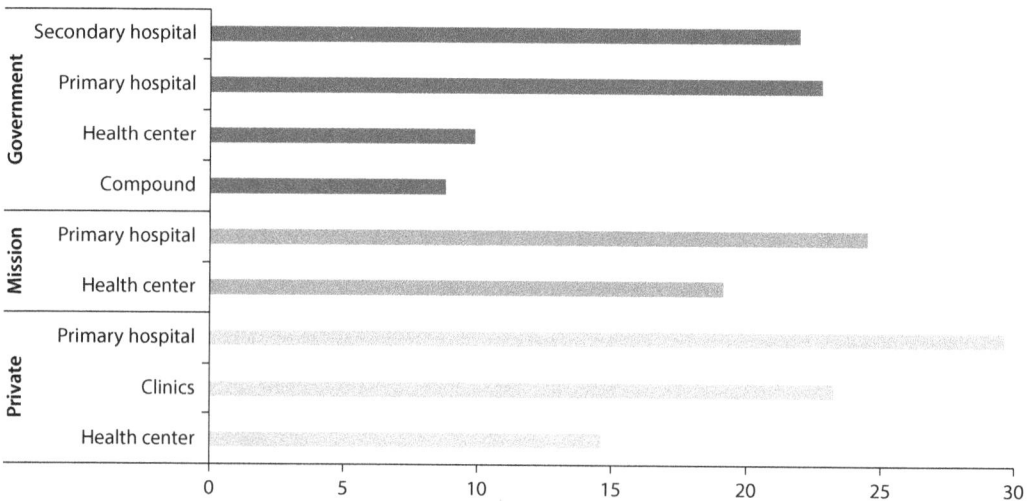

Source: Ghana NHIS claims expenditure in Volta region.

Figure 4.9 Per-Claim Expenditures, by Facility Type and Ownership, Inpatient Services

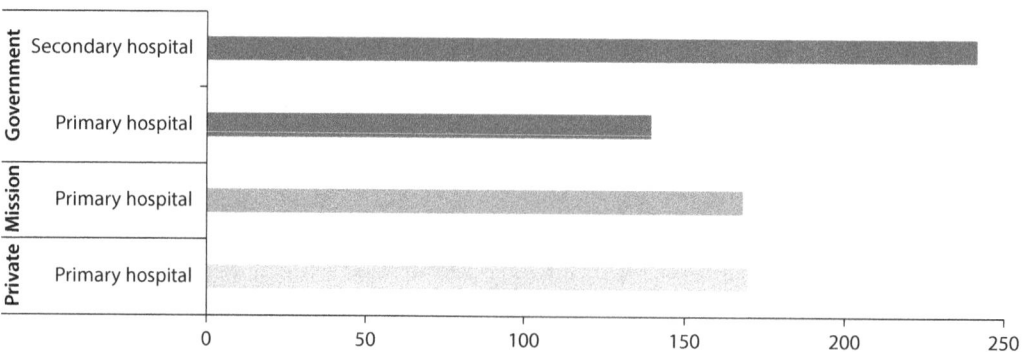

Source: Ghana NHIS claims expenditure in Volta region.

Claims expenditures vary significantly between individual facilities, even those of the same type. Per-claim expenditures for outpatient services at primary hospitals ranges from GH¢18 to GH¢112, a sixfold difference (figure 4.10). The median claim value for primary hospitals is GH¢24, and per-claim expenditures at the top five hospitals is at least 50 percent higher than the median. A similar but less drastic pattern is observed for inpatient services, per-claim expenditures for which range from GH¢121 to GH¢262), see figure 4.11.

Figure 4.10 Per-Claim Expenditure on Outpatient Services among Primary Hospitals

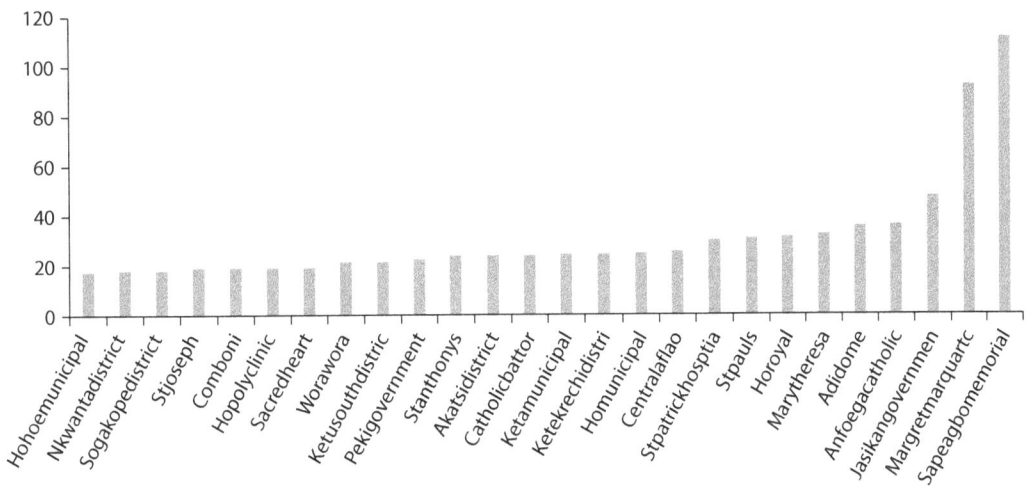

Source: Ghana NHIS claims expenditure in Volta region.

Figure 4.11 Per-Claim Expenditures on Inpatient Services among Primary Hospitals

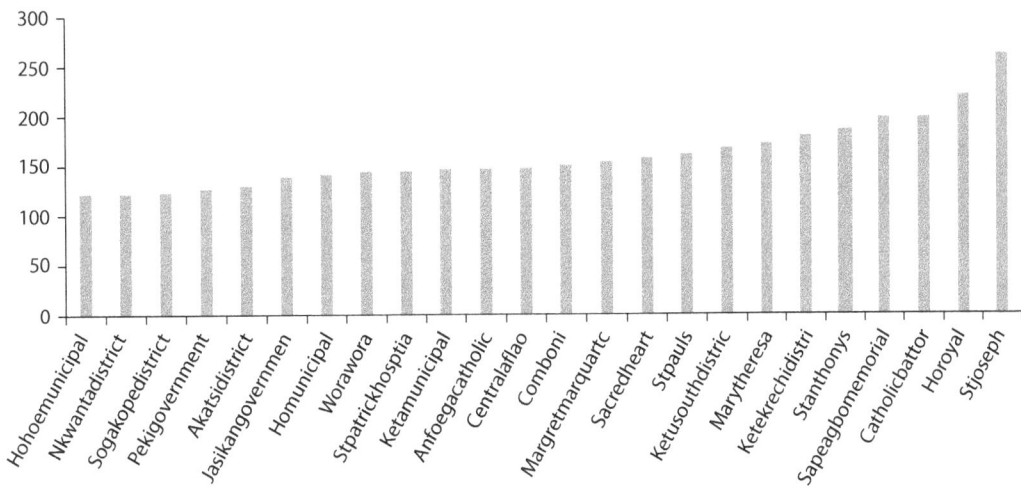

Source: Ghana NHIS claims expenditure in Volta region.

Claims Expenditure Distribution and Variation, by Member Characteristics

All NHIS members benefit from service reimbursements, but informal-sector workers, individuals over the age of 70, and children under the age of five benefit the most. Indigent individuals and dependent children are the only two categories for which the share of members exceeds the share of expenditures (figure 4.12). Members in all other categories receive a larger share of benefits than their share in total NHIS membership. Informal-sector workers are the only group that pays premiums, which may give them a stronger incentive to enroll when sick and seek care when enrolled. This group accounts for 30 percent of all members and 42 percent of total claims expenditure.

A small group of patients accounts for the majority of claims expenditures. The average number of outpatient visits among NHIS members in Volta who had been enrolled for at least 10 months in 2014 was 2.2 per year. However, 15 percent of members recorded at least 5 outpatient visits during the year, and this group accounted for more than half of total outpatient claims expenditures (figure 4.13). Another 16 percent recorded 3–4 visits during the year, and this group accounted for one-quarter of total claims expenditures. Only 8 percent of members recorded at least one hospital admission during 2014; among these patients, 17 percent were admitted 2 or more times

Figure 4.12 Benefit Incidence, by Membership Category, Volta, 2014

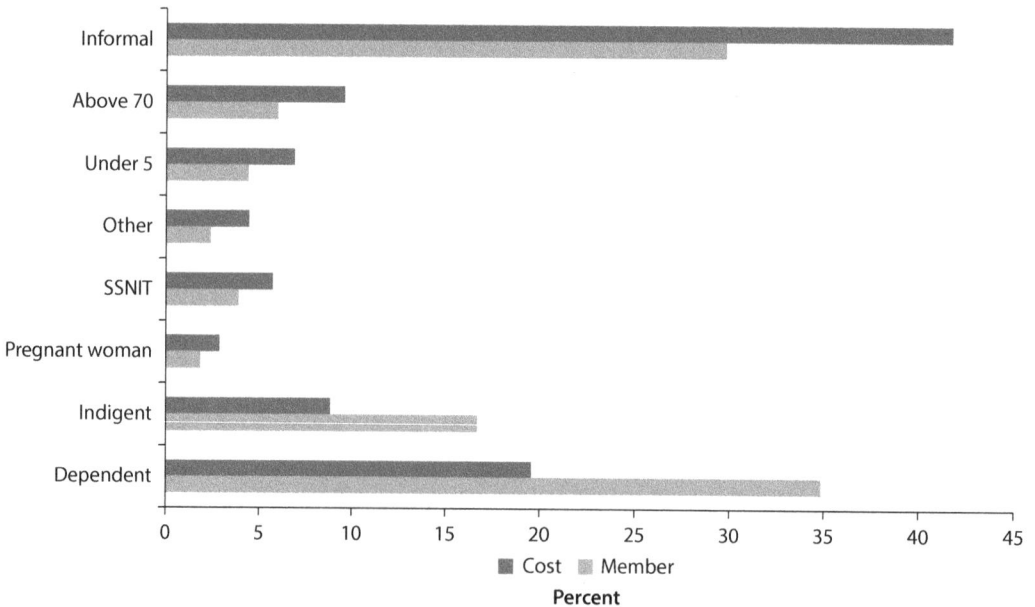

Source: Ghana NHIS claims expenditure in Volta region.

Figure 4.13 NHIS Members and Claims Expenditures, by Number of Outpatient Visits, Volta, 2014

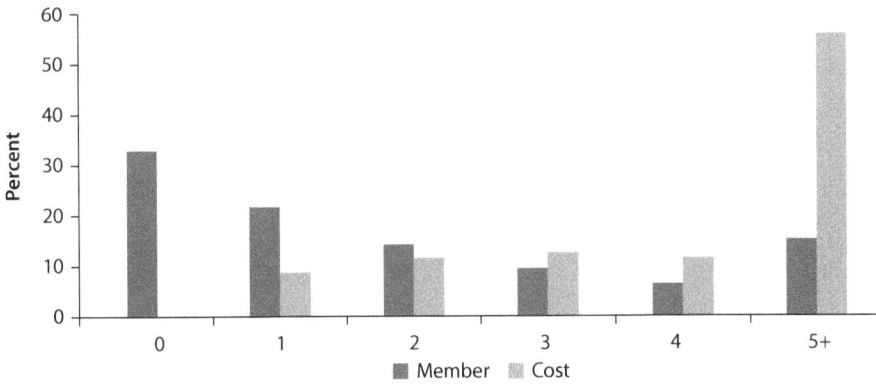

Source: Ghana NHIS claims expenditure in Volta region.

Figure 4.14 NHIS Members and Claims Expenditures, by Number of Inpatient Admissions, Volta, 2014

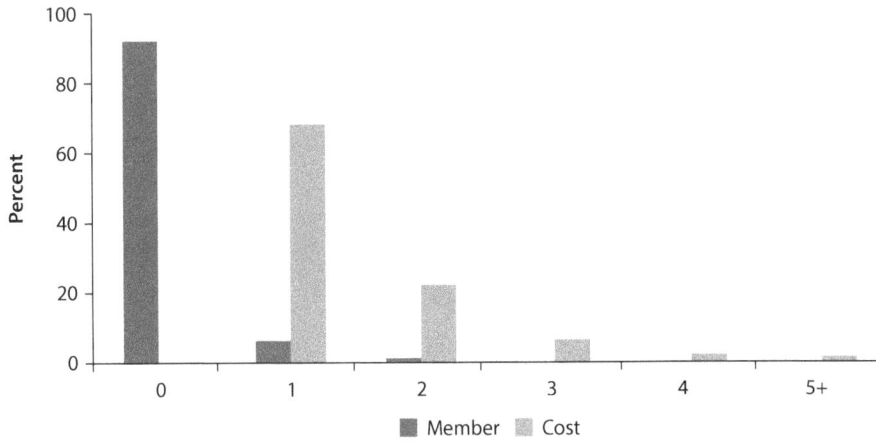

Source: Ghana NHIS claims expenditure in Volta region.

and accounted for about one-third of total inpatient claims expenditures (figure 4.14).

Average expenditure per member tends to increase with age. Children under five typically receive more medical care than older children, but after the age of 14, average expenditure per member rises steadily (figure 4.15). Average expenditures fall from GH¢46 for children under five to GH¢30 for the 5–14 group, then rise to a peak of GH¢104 for the 55–64 group. Spending on medicines drives this pattern, but inpatient services follow the same basic trajectory (figure 4.16).

Figure 4.15 Per-User Expenditures on Outpatient Services, by Age Group, Volta, 2014

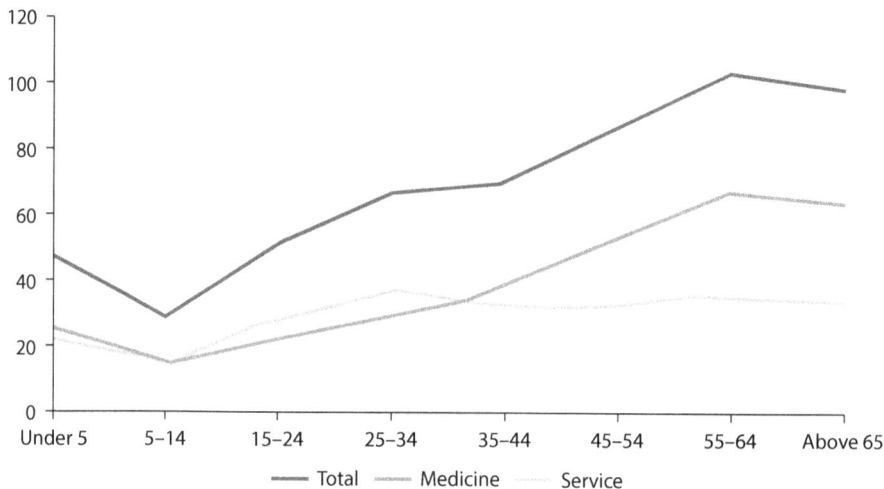

Legend: Total — Medicine — Service

Source: Ghana NHIS claims expenditure in Volta region.

Figure 4.16 Per-User Expenditures on Inpatient Services, by Age group, Volta, 2014

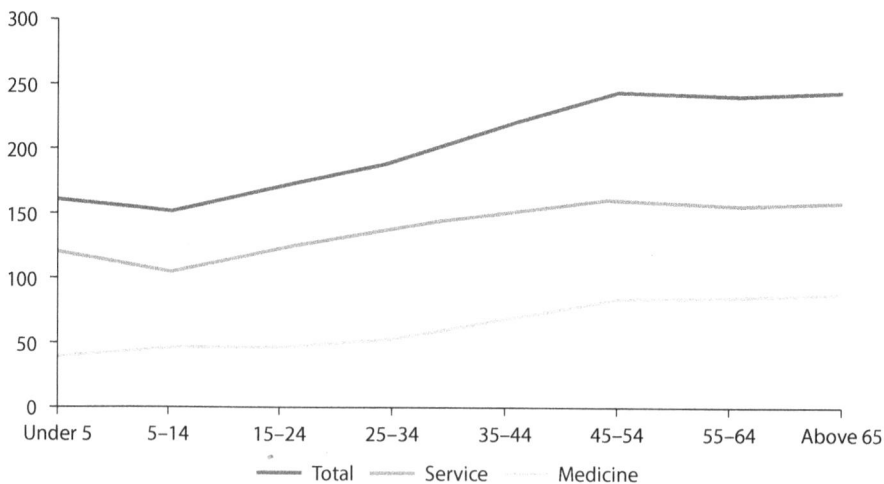

Legend: Total — Service — Medicine

Source: Ghana NHIS claims expenditure in Volta region.

The average claims expenditure per user also varies by membership category, as these categories correlate with socioeconomic status. In 2014, per user expenditures for both outpatient and inpatient services, medicine and medical services were highest among Social Security and National Insurance Trust (SSNIT) members who are formal-sector employees and wealthier individuals (figures 4.17 and 4.18). Meanwhile, per user expenditures were lowest among indigent individuals and informal-sector workers.

Figure 4.17 Per-User Expenditure on Outpatient Services, by Member Category, Volta, 2014

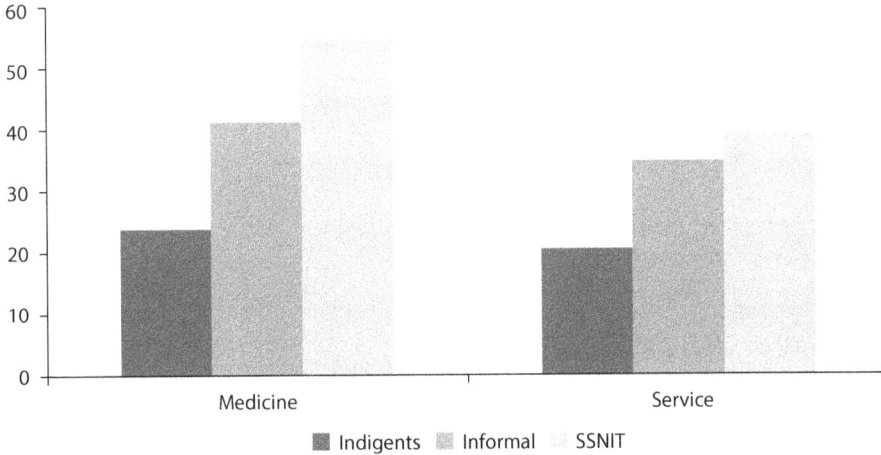

Source: Ghana NHIS claims expenditure in Volta region.

Figure 4.18 Per-User Expenditure on Inpatient Services, by Member Category, Volta, 2014

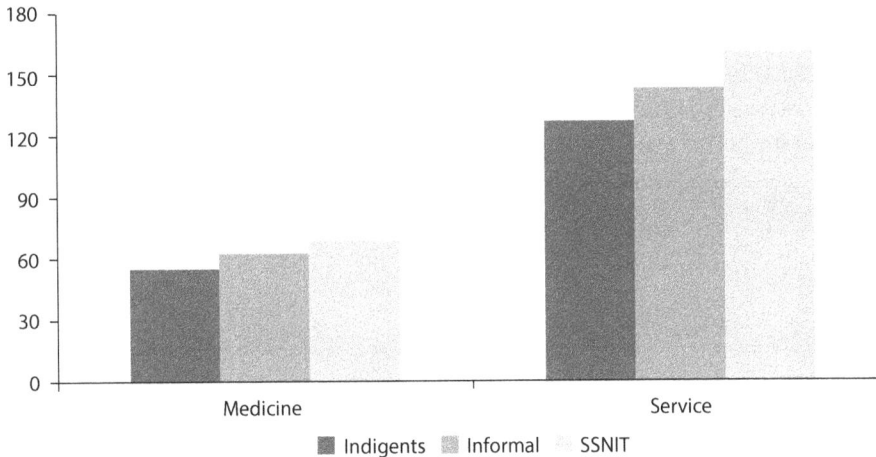

Source: Ghana NHIS claims expenditure in Volta region.

Examples of Potential Cost Saving Areas

Simulations based on claims-distribution data and per-claim expenditure data reveal several areas for potential cost savings. Prospective policy actions include encouraging the use of lower-cost providers, reducing variation in drug use, managing high cost cases and offering lower cost options (table 4.2). These simulations attempt to project the impact of various reforms, and policymakers should interpret their findings with caution.

Table 4.2 Simulated Savings from Redistributing Outpatient Claims Expenditures

	Potential savings (% of total outpatient claims expenditures in Volta)
Encouraging the use of lower-cost providers	
Assumption: A 50 percent shift in outpatient visits	
From government primary hospitals to government health centers	8.9
From private primary hospitals to private health centers	1.9
From private primary hospitals to government primary hospitals	0.8
From private primary hospitals to government health centers	2.4
From private clinics to government health centers	4.1
Assumption: An 80 percent shift in outpatient visits	
From government primary hospitals to government health centers	14.3
Adjusting prices	
Assumption: Reduced variation in prescription drug costs	
By aligning medicine costs in CHAG health centers with those in public health centers	1.5
Increasing the efficiency of patient visits	
Assumption: Reduced costs for returning patients	
By eliminating one outpatient visit among patients with at least five annual visits	11.2
Assumption: to offer group session as a lower cost option	
By shifting half of individual consultations to group consultations[a]	25

a. assumes the per-patient cost of group sessions to be half the cost of individual consultations.

Summary

Rising utilization rates, expanding coverage and higher unit costs are driving a persistent increase in claims expenditures. Between 2005 and 2008, the number of claims per NHIS member increased significantly. From 2008 to 2011, the rapidly growing number of NHIS members overtook utilization rates as the primary driver of rising claims expenditures, and in 2011, rising unit costs became the dominant force. This NHIS has not run a surplus since 2008, and in 2014 the deficit widened to GH¢300 million. The NHIA has recently turned to borrowing to finance the deficit, but without a structural realignment of revenues and expenditures, this strategy will prove unsustainable over the long term.

An in-depth analysis of the Volta region provides further insight into these dynamics. In Volta, outpatient visits account for 72 percent of claims expenditures. Medicine is the largest cost component of outpatient visits, representing more than half of outpatient claims expenditures. However, the high cost entailed by certain treatment types is the most important determinant of claims expenditures. Five groups of GDRGs account for 80 percent of the total claims cost in Volta: general outpatient consultations and treatments for conditions related to childbirth, infection, malaria, and hypertension.

Claims expenditure vary by provider type. Primary hospitals incur the largest share of claims costs, including 57 percent of outpatient expenditures and 90 percent of inpatient expenditures. Costs per claim are higher in hospitals and in non-public facilities. The cost of the average claim is 35 percent higher in private primary hospitals than in public primary hospitals, due in part to the higher reimbursement rates charged by non-public facilities. Nevertheless, Public facilities account for 53 percent of claims cost for both outpatient and inpatient visits.

The distribution of claims expenditures shows that all groups do not receive the same share of benefits relative to their share in total membership. Informal-sector workers receive the largest share of benefits relative to their share in total membership, while indigent individuals receive the smallest share. Indigent individuals also have the lowest cost per claim, while SSNIT members have the highest as they often seek care at more expensive facilities. The increasing cost of treating older patient cohorts can be observed across the age spectrum. While children under the age of five have higher per-patient costs than older children, costs increase steadily for all patients over the age of fourteen.

Note

1. The total claims cost is the number of members multiplied by the number of claims per member and by the average cost per claim.

CHAPTER 5

Factors Affecting Level and Efficiency of Claims Expenditures

Three factors determine the size and efficiency of claims expenditures in Ghana: coverage expansion, behaviors of service providers and National Health Insurance Scheme (NHIS) members, and the internal management of the National Health Insurance Authority (NHIA). Insurance intends to remove financial barrier for accessing care by expanding coverage. Policymakers' ability to influence this dimension is inherently limited. However, the authorities can affect the behavior of service providers and patients through measures to address adverse selection during enrollment, the suboptimal composition of the benefits package, low levels of cost-consciousness, and weak performance incentives. The NHIA can also enhance its own internal efficiency by reforming its systems for claims processing, provider oversight, and member engagement.

Behaviors of Service Providers and NHIS Members

Adverse Selection during Enrollment

Adverse selection is a major problem in insurance markets. High-risk individuals tend to have greater demand for insurance than low-risk individuals. Left unchecked, the tendency can threaten the stability of a national insurance program. An analysis of NHIS membership data reveals that adverse selection is increasing the cost of insurance.

NHIS members are more likely to be in high-risk age groups. Compared to national census data, the NHIS membership has a greater concentration of children under the age of five and individuals over the age of 55. These groups have significantly higher per-member health costs than those in the middle of the age range (figure 5.1).

There is a great deal of turnover among NHIS members. Out of all active members in January 2014, only 42 percent remained in the scheme in January 2015 (figure 5.2). This suggest that members may enroll during periods when they anticipate needing medical care, then leave the system once they have received that care. Moreover, members in high-risk age groups are more likely

Figure 5.1 Age Group Composition of Population Census, NHIS Member as of January 2014 and NHIS Members Continuously Enrolled for 12 Months

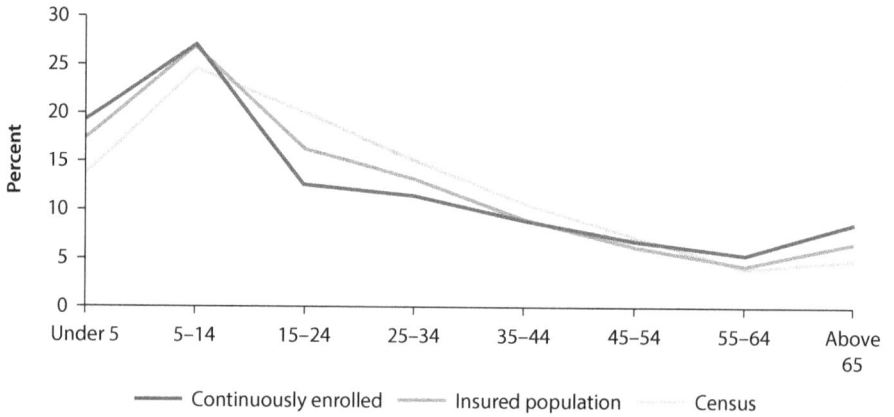

Source: Ghana NHIS membership data 2014 and Ghana Population Census data 2010.

Figure 5.2 NHIS Membership Attrition, January 2014–January 2015

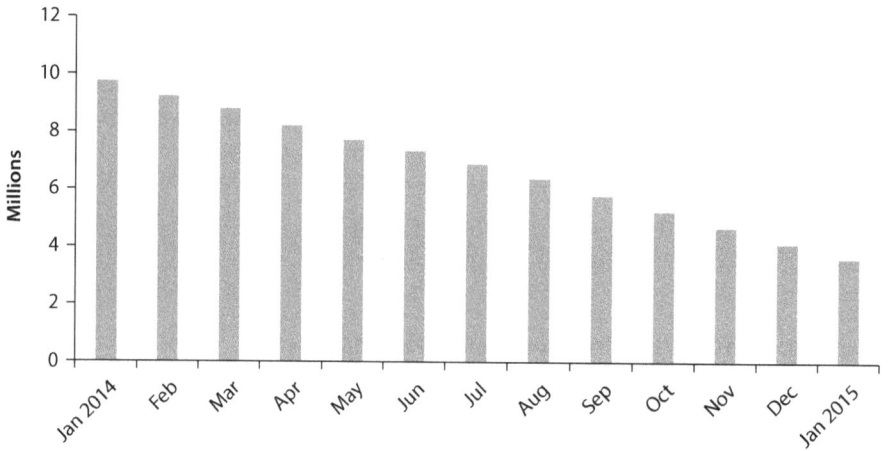

Source: Ghana NHIS membership data 2014.

to retain their membership (figure 5.3). Members aged 15–24, who have the lowest average medical costs of any age group, were the least likely to remain enrolled for a full 12 months. By January 2015, only 34.6 percent of members aged 15–24 remained in the program, compared to 46 percent of children under five and 53 percent for individuals over the age of 65. As a result, members who remained in the scheme used more medical services than those who dropped out (figure 5.4).

Tendency to Oversupply and Overuse Curative Services

The NHIS payment system does not promote cost-consciousness among service providers and encourages oversupply of services. Because health care facilities

Figure 5.3 Proportion of NHIS Members Continuously Enrolled for 12 Months in 2014, by Age Group

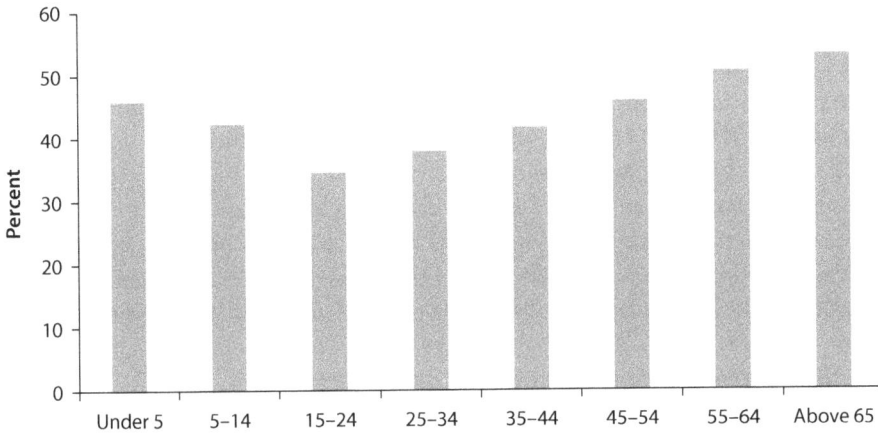

Source: Ghana NHIS membership data 2014.

Figure 5.4 Proportion of Members Utilizing Services in Volta, by Membership Renewal Tendency, 2014

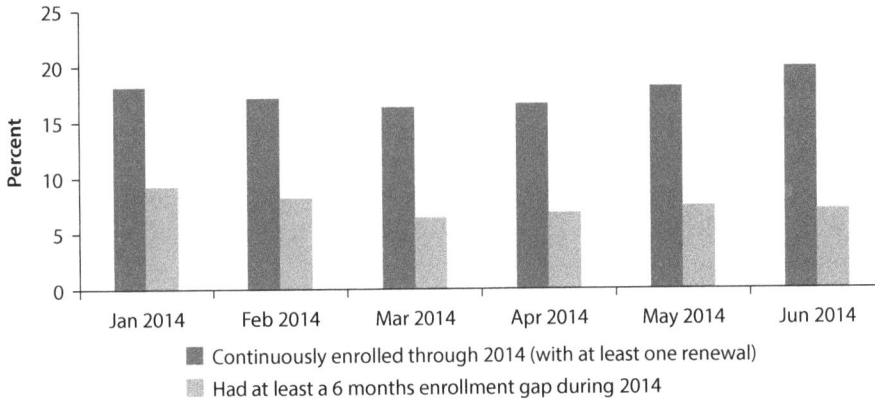

Source: Ghana NHIS membership data 2014 and NHIS claims data in Volta 2014.

typically rely on NHIS reimbursement to recover their operating expenses, they have no incentive to be efficient in claims expenditure. The capitation, fee-for-service (FFS) and Ghana diagnosis-related-group (GDRG)-based payment mechanisms used by NHIS do not incentivize providers to be efficient, and using an FFS system for pharmaceuticals encourages the use of prescription drugs. Consequently, 96 percent of claims in Volta include pharmaceutical expenditures. Diagnosis-related-groups (DRG) tariffs effectively function as a bundled FFS mechanism. While capitation payments do provide incentives to keep costs low by establishing a fixed reimbursement amount per member, this system only applies to outpatient primary care, which comprises less than one-third of total claims expenditures.

The government has contracted external loans to upgrade hospitals, and in the future these hospitals will be expected to finance their own operations, increasing the burden on an already-stretched NHIS. Based on information from the MoH and media reports, investment in ongoing projects amounts to at least US$1.4 billion, more than half of which is focused on secondary and tertiary facilities. Under the current financing system, more public resources will be allocated to these facilities through the MoH and NHIS, reducing the health sector's efficiency.

Generous benefit package and zero-copayment make it likely for patients to overuse. Insurance members in general are more likely to seek care when they face no explicit cost, sometimes necessary while sometimes unnecessary (referred as moral hazard). In addition, since it is zero copayment for all facilities, patients tend to choose higher level facilities that provide more expensive care.

Weak Incentives for Cost Effectiveness and Quality

NHIS covers later stages of health issues, which drives up claims expenditures. Although generous, NHIS benefit package does not explicitly cover preventive services. For example, NHIS covers outpatient, inpatient and emergency services, but not check-ups. NHIS covers childbirth, but not family planning; it covers malaria treatment, but not prevention. Many preventive programs are supported by donors or underfunded, and when preventive programs are ineffective, NHIS bears the cost. This issue can become more profound if there is no proper transition and booster for public health programs when donors withdraw their support.

NHIS reimburses private facilities at higher rates, but public facilities appear to be underutilized. The wage bill for public health workers reached Ghanaian cedi 1.5 billion in 2014, but the available data indicate that publicly financed health care workers only see an average of 2–2.9 outpatients per working day. Meanwhile, a large share of NHIS claims expenditures flows to private facilities.

Covering facility-based one-on-one model for provider-patient interaction does not encourage providers to offer low-cost alternatives. Currently, almost any visit to a health facility can be coded as an outpatient consultation eligible for reimbursement. More than half of claims expenditures are for general outpatient consultations, and 60 percent of outpatient expenditures occurs at hospitals. Because the NHIS covers hospital-based outpatient consultations, there is no incentive for providers to promote more cost-effective forms of consultation, such as group sessions for health education and chronic-disease management.

Ghana's health care financing system does not provide strong performance incentives either at the individual or facility level. Salaries and allowances for workers in public facilities are managed by the central government, and payment is not linked to either output or outcome indicators. NHIS provider payments are based on vetting reports and do not consider value of money. There is no mechanism to identify, publicize, or reward individuals and facilities that provide high-quality services or reduce health care costs. NHIS accreditation focuses on the quality of a facility's human resources, supplies, equipment, and infrastructure, but it does not directly capture service quality. Moreover, no service quality information is used to calibrate claims reimbursement, and there is no mechanism for rewarding providers that provide preventive services not included in the NHIS benefits package.

NHIA Internal Management

Inefficient Claims Processing

Claims processing by NHIA is labor-intensive and inefficient. Claims are vetted on an individual basis. Most claims are evaluated manually, even the relatively small share that are electronically submitted. The NHIA expends a staggering 1,200–4,800 staff weeks vetting each month's claims, and maintaining this schedule requires hundreds of staff members (table 5.1).

No estimates are available on the quality of claims vetting at the national level, but an analysis of claims in the Volta region suggests that the process is subject to significant errors. The Volta claims data reveal that 18 percent of submitted claims lack essential information or are submitted by unaccredited facilities (figure 5.5). These claims should have either been denied or returned to the facility for correction, yet unfulfilled claims represent just 3 percent of the value of all claims in Volta.

Table 5.1 Labor Requirements Simulation for Processing One Month's NHIS Claims

	Minutes spent on each claim	Staff weeks needed to process each month's claims	Staff members needed to process each month's claims
Scenario 1: One staff member vets 100 claims per day	4.8	4,800	1,200
Scenario 2: One staff member vets 200 claims per day	2.4	2,400	600
Scenario 3: One staff member vets 400 claims per day	1.2	1,200	300

Figure 5.5 Features of NHIS Claims Administration

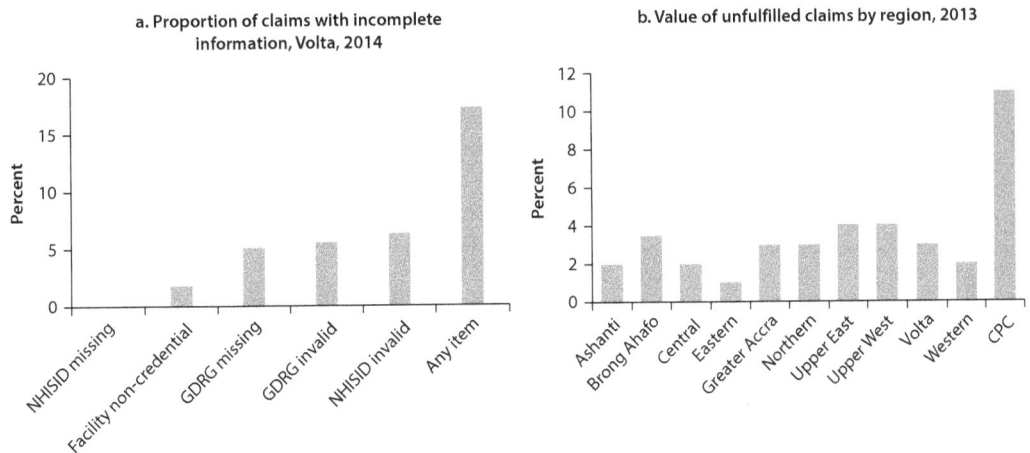

Source: Ghana NHIS claims data in Volta region for panel a, and NHIS presentation for panel b.

Inadequate Monitoring of Service Providers

Previous claims-expenditure reviews have shown that some service providers exhibit abnormal behavior that may indicate fraud or abuse and that warrants additional scrutiny. Private facilities, which tend to be high-cost providers, are more likely than other facilities to submit incomplete claims information. This is especially true for private primary hospitals (figure 5.6). Moreover, among private clinics that submit claims without GDRG information, 42 percent also lack diagnosis information, making it impossible to determine whether the GDRG is appropriate and these claims expenditure are eligible for reimbursement.

NHIA's claims-vetting system is not properly equipped to identify abnormal behavior among service providers. Claims offer a wealth of information on expenditure patterns, but most of the data captured by NHIA are not analyzed. There are three obstacles to using claims expenditures to identify abnormal provider behavior.

First, the existing data are not available in a format conducive to analysis. The Volta claims analysis was based on more than 3,000 individual Excel files submitted for 2014 alone. These files are not consistently formatted, and terms are used inconsistently (box 5.1). Addressing these issues is a costly and time-consuming process. While the NHIA has been working to develop standard templates, these issues remain common in all regions.

Second, the data captured by the current system are insufficient to verify the accuracy of the specified GDRG or appropriateness of the treatment. The NHIA

Figure 5.6 Share of Claims with Incomplete Information, by Facility Type and Ownership, Volta, 2014

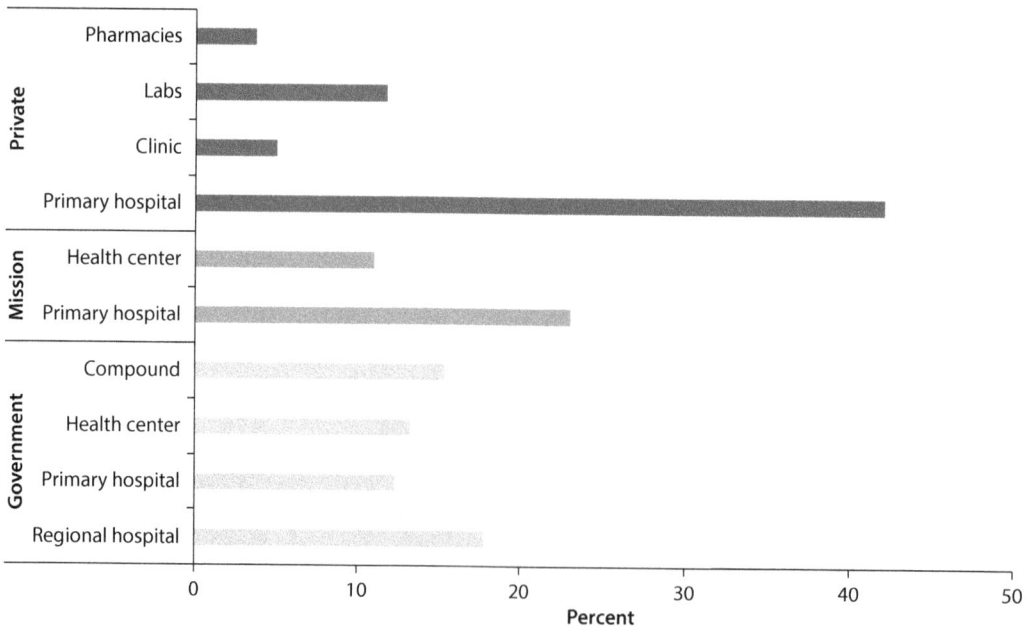

Source: Ghana NHIS claims data in Volta region.

requires facilities to submit a claims summary that includes the patient's membership identification number, GDRG, diagnosis, facility name, visit date, total cost, medicine cost and service cost. However, only one diagnosis is included for each claim, and no information on prescription drugs is included. Claims also lack information on patients' health status, which makes it difficult for NHIS to determine whether the diagnosis and GDRG coding were accurate and whether the treatment was appropriate.

Third, claims data are not integrated with other databases. Consequently, these data cannot be automatically cross-referenced against the membership database, the database of facility characteristics, or the overall health-management information system. This information can be compared manually with special efforts, but this is not a routine practice for the NHIA.

Insufficient Engagement with Members

There are limited opportunities for NHIS members to provide feedback on their experiences. After members visit health care facilities, claims are submitted under their names by facilities, but there is no interaction between members and NHIA. There is no standard mechanism for the NHIA to confirm receipt of services, service quality, payment problems, or any other issues encountered by the member. A call center was established as part of the Ghana National Health Insurance Project, but it does not seem to be playing a significant role in receiving feedback.

Box 5.1 Key Formatting Issues for NHIS Claims Data

There is no standard claims template. Within any given month, some claims use a single Excel file with separate worksheets for each specialty; some use one table that includes all services and specialties; some organize different tables by specialty in a single worksheet; and some use one file for each specialty. Providers do not use standard specialty titles and corresponding GDRG codes, and not all files or providers use standard table headings. The following table presents examples how headings in Microsoft Excel columns are different for same type of information.

NHIS identification number	Date of visiting	Age
NHISID	ADMISSION DATE	Age
NHIS ID	DATE OF ADMISSION	AGE
NHIS NO.	DATE	Age (yrs)
NHIS ID No.	A.DATE	AGE (Yrs)
NHISID No.	ATTEN.date	
NHIS ID NO.	ATTEND.date	
	ATTENDANCE.DATE	
	Attendance Date	
	DATE OF ATT.	

Without a mechanism to collect member feedback, NHIS claims information and beneficiary characteristics cannot be verified. Reimbursements are based on provider claims that are vetted through a manual desk review. There is no second source of information with which to verify claims. Without member engagement, false or erroneous claims are likely to go undiscovered.

The current system does not identify patients who seek care frequently, even though they represent a large share of claims expenditures. About 15 percent of NHIS members in Volta visit health care facilities at least five times during a given year, yet they account for more than half of total outpatient expenditures. Some of these patients suffer from chronic diseases, while others may be visiting multiple facilities in order to find the best care option. However, in some cases these repeat patients may reflect fraudulent claims. Developing systems to identify and track these patients could help improve the efficiency of claims expenditures and reduce errors and abuse.

CHAPTER 6

Designing Policies for Efficient Spending

This chapter provides recommendations to address the two major groups of factors affecting expenditure level and efficiency that are identified in chapter 5: behaviors of service providers and National Health Insurance Authority (NHIA) internal management. Behaviors of service providers are largely affected by designs and implementation of National Health Insurance Scheme (NHIS) policies such as enrollment, benefit package, provider payment mechanism and cost-sharing. By reforming these policies, perverse incentives for service providers and NHIS members may be addressed for improved efficiency of NHIS. More importantly, the implementation of these policy changes need to be supplemented with improvement in NHIA's capacity in managing expenditures so that behaviors of service providers and members can be monitored and affected.

Recommendations

Addressing Perverse Incentives among Service Providers and NHIS Members

The enrollment process should be refined to address adverse selection. Because the NHIS is primarily financed by taxes, it should not attempt to exclude high-cost individuals in order to address adverse selection. However, the NHIS must provide incentives for low-cost individuals to enroll and remain within the scheme. While this will not necessarily lead to decrease in total claims expenditures in short term, it will form a steady membership base for NHIS to actively engage, which will be necessary to expand preventive programs and reduce future claims expenditures.

There are several ways in which NHIS can incentivize enrollment by younger, healthier individuals. Year-round enrollment should be replaced by restricted enrollment periods, with exceptions for major life events such as marriage or pregnancy. The NHIA should work to make enrollment less difficult by hiring more staff and providing better training and equipment. The enrollment process may also incorporate simple health tests (e.g. blood-pressure monitoring) and health-education group sessions to proactively engage with the health of new members. Finally, it may be necessary to impose fees on members who drop out of the scheme.

The NHIA should rationalize its benefits package. The international experience underscores the importance of (a) adopting a positive list of included benefits rather than a negative list of excluded conditions, (b) gradually expanding the benefits package to manage cost increases and implementation challenges, and (c) creating a straightforward institutional process for adjusting the benefits plan. Key concerns that should inform the design of the benefits package include its financial cost and budgetary impact, the number of people affected, the severity of the health conditions addressed, its effect on household budgets, equity concerns, and ethical implications.

Adopting a positive list of benefits entails several important advantages. Many Latin American countries have had positive experiences with explicit benefits packages, which can help improve communication with members, empower patients during their interactions with health providers, and focus resources on the most cost-effective interventions. Concentrating on a relatively narrow range of services can also improve service quality. Adopting a positive benefits package and gradually expanding the range of services it covers could assist NHIS in assuming responsibility for providing preventive services that are currently supported by donors if needed.

NHIA should incentivize innovative service-delivery models as an alternative to hospital-based one-on-one interactions. Global experiences suggest that changing service delivery mode can yield significant savings, e.g., shifting inpatient procedures to outpatient settings, mailing drugs and consultations over phone. Lower-cost delivery models are especially important for patients in the top five Ghana diagnosis-related-groups (GDRGs): outpatient consultations, malaria, infection, childbirth, and hypertension. One option is to shift service use from hospitals to lower level facilities (e.g., health centers and CHPS compounds) and communities when supply conditions allow. Another option is to engage members on a group basis before they seek individual treatment. For example, facilities may offer group consultation sessions and drug refill sessions for cost savings.

Cost-sharing arrangements can promote cost-consciousness among NHIS members and discourage the overuse of health services. Cost-sharing mechanisms include copayments (a fixed amount for each service), coinsurance (a fixed percentage of the total claim amount), and deductibles (a fixed amount that patients must pay for services before insurance benefits apply). These are often used, with exemptions to the poor, in order to prevent people initiate unnecessary care due to the lower price of services related to health insurance coverage. Copayment and coinsurance mechanisms are often used in tiers for different level of services or pharmaceuticals, creating incentives for members to use more cost-effective services. Copayments for brand-name drugs are typically higher than those for generic drugs and higher for hospitals than for local health facilities. As demand for private providers remains strong even when public providers are underutilized, establishing higher copayments for private providers can encourage patients to seek care at public facilities. Copayments can also be used to promote group sessions as an alternative to one-on-one consultations.

Reimbursement mechanisms should be redesigned to increase providers' cost consciousness and maximize value for money. Broadening the treatment areas to which capitation payments apply (e.g., pharmaceutical prescriptions, inpatient services) would discourage providers from shifting financial risks to fee-for-service and GDRG-based payment mechanisms. In cases where capitation payments are not feasible, total expenditures should be capped. GDRG tariff rates and pharmaceutical prices should be negotiated on an aggregate basis. However, policymakers must take steps to ensure that these measures do not prompt service providers to increase financial pressure on patients.

The NHIS should explicitly incentivize preventive services. Providing similar capitation payments for both low-cost preventive services and high-cost curative services would encourage health care providers to focus on the former. Education and outreach can help boost demand for preventive services such as immunizations and disease screening. Linking to overall health financing system, these measures should be put in place in coordination with the country's transition plan for donor-financed preventive health programs.

Payment mechanisms should promote high service quality. Many countries use performance-based payment systems to improve service quality. These systems can be phased-in gradually, either by geographic region or by service level. Quality indicators should be jointly determined with providers and based on reliable data. For example, as malaria cases account for about one-third of claims, malaria-diagnosis accuracy (which is currently measured by MoH) would be a potential metric for service quality. Other prospective quality indicators include absenteeism, adherence to clinical guidelines, responsiveness to patients, peer-review performance, and patient feedback. NHIA clinical audits are essentially practicing this idea, but they only apply to claims that are under investigation.

Measures must be taken for risk adjustment in payment mechanisms to prevent adverse consequences for patients in need of more expensive forms of care. Unless the case mix can be adjusted in payment mechanism, cost-conscious providers may attempt to deny care to patients requiring costly services. Many OECD countries have accumulated experiences in risk adjustment for diagnosis-related-groups, capitation and global budget. Demographic profiles are often indicators to begin with for risk adjustment, with expenditure history and drug history being incorporated at later stage.

Enhancing Expenditure Management at the NHIA

The NHIA's electronic claims-processing system should be expanded and refined. The information provided by this system is significantly better than the summary data submitted in Excel files. However, the system covers just 8 percent of total claims. Moreover, only the submission stage is electronic, and the vetting process remains manual. In addition, the data on the NHIA server can only be accessed by special request. An enhanced electronic claims-processing system should have increased capacity, algorithms for automated vetting, and linkages to other public health databases.

NHIA should regularly analyze patterns of service utilization and service quality by service provider and member characteristics. Regular analysis would enable the NHIA to identify providers that exhibit abnormal behavior patterns and members who frequently seek care so that follow-up actions can be taken to promote greater expenditure efficiency. With an enhanced claims system in place, greater capacity for statistical analysis would strengthen the NHIA's ability to combat waste and fraud, and it would bolster the analytical foundation for future reforms. The international experience shows that the mere fact that effective oversight mechanisms are in place tends to encourage compliance with regulations, obviating the need for aggressive interventions. Information on provider performance can also be used as a basis for contract negotiations or to establish ranking systems designed to improve service quality by encouraging competition.

A comprehensive framework for member engagement could improve the quality of interactions between the NHIA and its members. New members should have basic health risks assessed at enrollment, and outreach efforts should begin immediately. Members should be encouraged to seek preventive care. The NHIA should actively verify information and solicit feedback on their experiences with health care providers through periodic surveys or tele-communication applications. Special case-management programs should be established to target patients who seek frequent care in order to optimize their care seeking.

Areas for Further Analytical Work

The NHIA should collect more comprehensive information on interactions between patients and health care providers. Beyond the basic information needed to process claims, the NHIA should record patients' health status, any tests undertaken, any procedures performed, the results of lab work, any medicines prescribed, and any out-of-pocket costs incurred. This information will enable the NHIA to more effectively judge the appropriateness of diagnoses, claims coding, and treatment plans. This will also help the NHIA adjust the case mix while paying providers.

Further analysis will be necessary for NHIS to spend more efficiently. Monitoring the effects—both intended and unintended—of cost-containment policies will be essential to their successful implementation. In addition, policymakers require more detailed information on out-of-pocket spending in the health care sector, particularly by NHIS members. A thorough assessment of existing systems for measuring and assuring service quality in health sector would help identify priority areas for intervention, particularly in primary care. Further research will also be necessary to develop a system for building risk profiles for NHIS members and designing risk-adjusted payment mechanisms. Piloting group information and treatment sessions for certain GDRGs and comparing their cost-effectiveness to one-on-one interactions will require significant analytical capacity, as will the completion of a feasibility study on case-management programs for patients that frequently seek care. Finally, there is a pressing need to develop a framework for collaborating with the private sector based on a comprehensive assessment of private facilities' service costs, focus areas, and complementarities with public providers.

Environmental Benefits Statement

The World Bank Group is committed to reducing its environmental footprint. In support of this commitment, we leverage electronic publishing options and print-on-demand technology, which is located in regional hubs worldwide. Together, these initiatives enable print runs to be lowered and shipping distances decreased, resulting in reduced paper consumption, chemical use, greenhouse gas emissions, and waste.

We follow the recommended standards for paper use set by the Green Press Initiative. The majority of our books are printed on Forest Stewardship Council (FSC)–certified paper, with nearly all containing 50–100 percent recycled content. The recycled fiber in our book paper is either unbleached or bleached using totally chlorine-free (TCF), processed chlorine–free (PCF), or enhanced elemental chlorine–free (EECF) processes.

More information about the Bank's environmental philosophy can be found at http://www.worldbank.org/corporateresponsibility.

green press INITIATIVE

www.ingramcontent.com/pod-product-compliance
Lightning Source LLC
Chambersburg PA
CBHW080003280326
41935CB00013B/1735